# The SEO Battlefield

*Winning Strategies for*
*Search Marketing Programs*

*Anne Ahola Ward*

Beijing · Boston · Farnham · Sebastopol · Tokyo

**The SEO Battlefield**

by Anne Ahola Ward

Printed in the United States of America.

Published by O'Reilly Media, Inc., 1005 Gravenstein Highway North, Sebastopol, CA 95472.

O'Reilly books may be purchased for educational, business, or sales promotional use. Online editions are also available for most titles (*http://oreilly.com/safari*). For more information, contact our corporate/institutional sales department: 800-998-9938 or *corporate@oreilly.com*.

**Editor:** Meg Foley
**Production Editor:** Nicholas Adams
**Copyeditor:** Gillian McGarvey
**Proofreader:** Charles Roumeliotis

**Indexer:** Judy McConville
**Interior Designer:** David Futato
**Cover Designer:** Randy Comer
**Illustrator:** Rebecca Demarest

April 2017:        First Edition

**Revision History for the First Edition**
2017-03-21:    First Release

See *http://oreilly.com/catalog/errata.csp?isbn=9781491958377* for release details.

978-1-491-95837-7

[LSI]

*I dedicate this book to my late, great father, J. David Ahola.*

*As one of the leading internal forensic fraud examiners and top dads in the country, my father taught me valuable life lessons that molded me into the woman I am today.*

*A portion of the proceeds of this book will go towards the J. David Ahola Memorial Internal Audit Scholarship (http://jdavidahola.com) at Bauer College of Business, University of Houston.*

# Table of Contents

# Foreword

Technology and visions of the future have always beguiled me, even in my earliest memories. My first computer was a Commodore 64 that I shared with my brother at around age five or six. Throughout my childhood, computers were ever-present—my dad always made sure of that. My parents encouraged me to pursue whatever interested me throughout my life, so I did. Sometimes my interests seemed a bit odd to others. At age seven, I wanted to reinvent the diaper to be ecofriendly and made of leaves. This was probably inspired by *Gilligan's Island* reruns. At age nine, I disassembled and reassembled my clock radio to see how it worked. In junior high school, I sewed a watch onto a T-shirt for my science fair project invention. The project was not well received. *I was told nobody would ever want to wear a gadget.*

I constantly tinkered with every piece of technology I could get my hands on, trying to learn more. My fascination with the "interwebs" started the moment that sweet, sweet 28.8 Cardinal modem came into my life. I discovered Compuserve and AOL search, then chat rooms. Fondly I remember visiting the undergraduate library at University of Texas and cruising the web. Lycos, Alta Vista, Excite, Yahoo!, and Geocities were my bridge to another planet. Information became rapidly available like never before and my fascination with the virtual world bloomed.

After high school, I attended the University of Texas at Austin during the first dotcom boom in the late 1990s. It was a truly exciting time for a tech person, because startups began appearing everywhere overnight, even in lil' old Austin. In college, I dabbled as one should. I *sort of* tried to start a record label, sold health supplements and knives (separately) for two seconds, managed records for a museum, and then became their DBA. My first "tech job" was as a DBA, but it was a joyless enterprise. Alas, the web beckoned.

I very badly moonlighted while in the university system to also become an HTML editor at iBooks. This decision to straddle both cost me a lot; I underestimated my "easiest" class, showing up only three times during the whole semester, and thus failing what should have been a ridiculously easy required credit. Don't worry—to the happiness of my family, I did eventually graduate, but it was an interesting journey!

iBooks.com converted books for various publishers from Quark to Pagemaker and then onto the web. O'Reilly Media was their biggest client by far. We didn't have any friendly, glossy WYSIWYG tools in 2000—we barely had Dreamweaver. I still believe that BBEdit hacks were my ultimate savior until I learned about more advanced scripting languages. Most people had CRT displays in 2000, and *nobody* wanted to read books on them. Had the screen hardware been more advanced in 2000, I think that startup would have been far more successful.

Like many people learning something new, I was not a particularly great web developer at first. While working away at night as an HTML editor, I was also *reading the books* while I converted them and tidied up the images. There was a sizable library of O'Reilly books laying around at the office and anyone could pick them up, so I did. Reading those books changed the course of my career and life dramatically. Not only did I learn how to build cool things on the web, but I began to understand all the pieces of the WWW and how they came together. As a trailblazer and futurist enthusiast, I was soon to *discover search* as a "thing to do." It wasn't always.

I believe that search is both a tool and a key to life in technology. Connectivity to information is so, so important. Search happens in way more places than the browser. For example, I met my husband in late 2000 simply because he did a search for a band called Silverchair that had incredibly poor SEO. They'd created a fan chat module named Silver Chat that they didn't yet rank for. I was a member of the *telnet* silverchat, not the band-created one. It was a private telnet-based group in Austin, which was where he was moving, so he joined it just for kicks. They met in the meatspace every week, we both went the same week, and the rest is history. So technically I met my soulmate because of a 90s band's inadequate SEO.

Becoming a designer and developer contractor for Apple education in enterprise marketing changed the course of my career forever. With my two lady hands, I helped build the first Apple education community right before iTunes was launching. A whole geeky, heady world of marketing was revealed to me that I never knew existed: *website marketing.*

The web was more than a place to put your information; it was a storefront, a way to consume new content. I saw what happened when demand was so amazingly high that the Apple store crumbled for hours. While I was at Apple, iTunes launched, which was intoxicating for an aspiring geek. When podcasts became "a thing," it was a wonderful world. After leaving Apple, it became clear to me that I needed to be the person who decided what was on the front of the page rather than behind it. Tools had gotten better by that point, so I lost interest.

The problem was (at first) that deciding what was on the front of the page wasn't really a full-time job, *yet!* The key to finding a career in search was my endless passion for tinkering and testing. Once analytics became available—even just the site traffic numbers—it was over. The courtship was short-lived. Through my fascination with analytics, I started to become what is now considered to be an SEO (or a *growth hacker*).

Back in 2005, I was doing "web stuff." Companies hired me professing to want SEO done, but nobody actually knew what it meant. Quite often companies would conflate web development with SEO; everyone wanted it but nobody knew what it really was.

I started my own firm in 2009 and haven't looked back. During my tenure as an agency SEO lead, I've helped many startups become enterprises. My team has also grown. When people tell me they want to know what I know—while flattering—it makes me wonder how to best help curious search adventurers of the world move forward.

And here we are today—sweet! This book is the culmination of many years of experience in the field and my desire to help get marketers and developers excited about search domination. I hope that sharing the lessons I've learned will help you become a stronger search marketer and solve potential problems you might have in the future.

# Preface

## About This Book

As I sat down to write this book, I realized there were many things to consider. I wanted to write a book to help people from many different disciplines enact SEO programs effectively. My goal was to educate both developers and marketers on the most important things to consider when improving search dominance.

If you've never really heard of SEO and have no marketing or technical experience, then you may want to read other awesome O'Reilly (*http://www.oreilly.com*) books on these topics first.

My career has been spent in web development, design, interpreting analytics, and practicing SEO. This hybrid nature has resulted in a more technical search marketing book than many others out there on the market. I'm not going to tell you how to write good content; I'm going to help you optimize for what search engine relevancy truly means.

This book is ideal for marketing teams who need to be hybrids and cover more ground in terms of understanding search. Publicly traded companies and larger companies and startups alike will benefit from the SEO frameworks I've laid out.

## Conventions Used in This Book

The following typographical conventions are used in this book:

*Italic*
> Indicates new terms, URLs, email addresses, filenames, and file extensions.

`Constant width`
> Used for program listings, as well as within paragraphs to refer to program elements such as variable or function names, databases, data types, environment variables, statements, and keywords.

**`Constant width bold`**
> Shows commands or other text that should be typed literally by the user.

*`Constant width italic`*
> Shows text that should be replaced with user-supplied values or by values determined by context.

This element signifies a tip or suggestion.

This element signifies a general note.

This element indicates a warning or caution.

# O'Reilly Safari

 *Safari* (formerly Safari Books Online) is a membership-based training and reference platform for enterprise, government, educators, and individuals.

Members have access to thousands of books, training videos, Learning Paths, interactive tutorials, and curated playlists from over 250 publishers, including O'Reilly Media, Harvard Business Review, Prentice Hall Professional, Addison-Wesley Professional, Microsoft Press, Sams, Que, Peachpit Press, Adobe, Focal Press, Cisco Press, John Wiley & Sons, Syngress, Morgan Kaufmann, IBM Redbooks, Packt, Adobe Press, FT Press, Apress, Manning, New Riders, McGraw-Hill, Jones & Bartlett, and Course Technology, among others.

For more information, please visit *http://oreilly.com/safari*.

# How to Contact Us

Please address comments and questions concerning this book to the publisher:

O'Reilly Media, Inc.
1005 Gravenstein Highway North
Sebastopol, CA 95472
800-998-9938 (in the United States or Canada)
707-829-0515 (international or local)
707-829-0104 (fax)

We have a web page for this book, where we list errata, examples, and any additional information. You can access this page at *http://bit.ly/the-seo-battlefield*.

To comment or ask technical questions about this book, send email to *bookques tions@oreilly.com*.

For more information about our books, courses, conferences, and news, see our website at *http://www.oreilly.com*.

Find us on Facebook (*http://facebook.com/oreilly*)

Follow us on Twitter (*http://twitter.com/oreillymedia*)

Watch us on YouTube (*http://www.youtube.com/oreillymedia*)

# Acknowledgments

*My warmest and sincerest heartfelt thanks to:*

Georgina Ahola, my Mom who has loved and supported me feverishly since my birth. She is my #1 fan! Throughout the writing process she kept asking me "how many pages?" knowing I'd dutifully report back, even when I didn't want to, which pushed me forward.

My husband Joel "Val" Ward, the ultimate mad *data scientist*—the wind beneath my wings, a marvelous tech editor, my best friend, and undisputed soul mate. I couldn't have done this without his support.

Tyler Durrett, a top-notch tech editor who has been a close creative collaborator for many years. His support and overall acceptance for my moments of weirdness kept me going when the weeks grew so, so long.

Meg Foley, my amazing editor at O'Reilly and TV twin, whose support and willingness to laugh at my jokes made all of this more fun.

Lastly, but not least, a big thank you to my compatriots, heroes, and friends. All of you who believed in me, rooted for me, and were there for me when I needed you. Thank you. For that you are very cool.

# CHAPTER 1

# Welcome to the Battlefield

Virtual war wages every day. Dynasties rise and fall on the heels of search engine algorithm changes. What you're fighting for in terms of SEO ground isn't actually ground, it's quicksand.

The way a company appears in search can alter its course and determine outcomes. When search is not properly attended to, a company puts itself at risk: competition can swoop in, reputations get tarnished. By neglecting to update your company's information online, it can inadvertently funnel people to your competitors or bad actors.

## Introduction

The practice of search engine optimization is inherently competitive *yet* fair because nobody maintains top positions forever. Change is an uninterrupted force. Search is akin to a battlefield, because SEO warriors must continually empire-build or risk losing it all. Companies rarely maintain search prominence without sagacious exertion and commitment. Just like life and love, search is a battlefield.

> Wake early if you want another man's life or land. No lamb for the lazy wolf. No battles fought in bed.
>
> —The Hávamál (*http://genes.mit.edu/burgelab/vikingquotes.htm*), Old Norse

Coveted search rankings do not happen by accident. If you want to rank in the top entries consistently, you must work tirelessly. Exalted kings of search are a rarity. Even if you're friends with a Hollywood legend, search dominance is far from a guarantee. You could get lucky—maybe you're caught in a news cycle—but do you really want to depend on luck?

How do we define search? Searching signals *the intention to explore information* via search engines. Search can do so much for us: make fortunes, help convict murderers, connect lost relatives, and manipulate political elections. To understand and then anticipate what people will explore online seems like magic for some people. But there's no magic in SEO; it only seems that way from the outside because the actions taken are completely unpredictable. Search is the gateway to the bounteous information held within the web, the Giant Global Graph (see "All SERPs Are Not the Same" on page 126), and thus the internet as a whole.

Building a successful SEO program means being realistic about your resources, automating what you can when you can, and experimenting all of the time. Try to learn from those experiments. The thing about having gumption is that its presence does not guarantee successful outcomes. SEO programs are doomed to fail when they don't quickly recognize what's not working or when they get bogged down in minutiae, but hey, that's more billable hours, right? (Kidding!)

Search optimization continues to happen everywhere whether or not you take notice. When you're searching for something as simple as a person's name, it's fairly rare to not see various social media listings dominating page one. Sites like Facebook, Yelp, or LinkedIn easily own the top search listing on a search engine result page (SERP) for a person's name or business. If a person is not internet-active, then arbitrageurs or sites like Spokeo and White Pages will successfully rank their name. Common names often have expanded paid and organic results such as listings pages on LinkedIn or paid ads for background checks, alumni, or finding public records.

You can lose significant ground to a competitor for a highly lucrative search term if you do not invest in SEO, or at least stay aware of it. It's imperative to remain aware of how you appear online in today's business world and to the vast majority of society. One scenario that can happen if you do not pay attention to your site's SEO is that an arbitrageur will creep into the space. Arbitrageurs work to rank for what *you* want to rank for and then sell it back to you (or anyone else who will pay). Arbitrageurs are like ghost ships playing an extravagant game of Monopoly. I've seen expensive online usurping happen to companies who lag behind, and it's an unfortunate price to pay for a slow market-reaction time.

In order to grow a website's presence, constant effort must be expended. Elements of both offense and defense strategies should coexist symbiotically in all search programs. SEOs and growth hackers *alike* make moves with poles-apart tactics and maneuvers. Everyone can make a place on the virtual chess search board. What *you* choose to do about it is up to you. I say *own it*.

Organizations with a lack of SEO mindfulness can easily become dependent on costly paid search traffic for revenue. Paid traffic takes many forms: affiliate marketing, retargeting, geo, local, mobile, etc. Paid is not a contradistinctive force to organic search. There are many fiscal benefits to paid search when it is done right, especially in the realms of retargeting or social. Mixing organic and paid search can yield interesting fruit. There are different areas of battle; prepare for all paths: instead of "one if by land, and two if by sea," the true professional covers both. Diversification of promotional assets allows for the deepest penetration. It's been shown countless times that people gain more trust in a company if they see its name mentioned twice or more in a search result.

There are more search engines and methods for a site to be found than a simple Bing search. Worrying about only one engine and method of search is certainly the easiest thing to do, but it's not necessarily the best. Many SEO programs fail because they forget to variegate. For example, I've been watching this new socially focused eco-friendly browser Ecosia take off slowly but surely since 2013. Ecosia is fun to use and returns generally useful results. I love that my search queries are planting trees! I'm at 1,758 and counting.

At the time of writing this book, Ecosia's traffic can seem insignificant statistically if Google is the only foil for success. A portion of the proceeds of Ecosia's ads go towards planting trees in Africa and beyond; they surpassed four million trees in early 2016. The ads platform runs on Yahoo! and Bing's network. It all started when the CEO and founder of Ecosia, Christian Kroll, read a book about the importance of rainforests and decided he had no choice but to take action. He started Ecosia's predecessor Forestle in 2008, which was managed in partnership with Google. The project quickly took off and started to take flight, but then it shut down suddenly in 2011.

The stories about Forestle's demise are markedly different, but many agree it was a success. Some people believe that Forestle's success is precisely why its partnership with Google abruptly ended. Years later, Kroll started Ecosia with the same mission as Forestle—to raise funds to tackle the problem of deforestation. And now, many people are starting to notice this engine. It doesn't pay to ignore seedlings; anything can happen. The internet is a magical place. If we look at the competitive data, Ecosia's growth trajectory is significantly higher MOM (Figures 1-1 and 1-2).

| Recent Sites | Unique Visitors | MOM% |
|---|---|---|
| google.com | 185,197,295 | 0.52% |
| ecosia.org | 97,013 | 86.47% |

*Figure 1-1. David versus Goliath? Right column shows growth month over month, April 2016.*

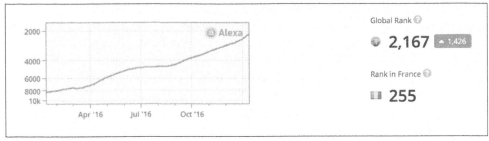

*Figure 1-2. Alexa shows growth since April 2016, trending sharply up in global rank.*

Yes, Ecosia (*https://en.wikipedia.org/wiki/Ecosia*) is based on Bing, but anything could happen. There are many rising stars in tech. New empires will form in search. Entirely new platforms and methods of search will start to exist and evolve with the proliferation of IoT and the Nth screen (see Chapter 8).

Vigilant search mavens don't take what's handed to them on industry blogs; they seek out and watch the Christian Krolls of the world, because he could be the next Steve Jobs.

Search can be text, voice, images, or video and that's about to change. This is one of the most exciting times to perform search optimization! The more screens and connectivity we see, the more important our SEO existence will become. Companies will always need experts to help them navigate ways to present themselves on the web. *SEO is here to stay.*

Now that we've talked moon shots, let's talk about the Google. We know a few things about Google's founders. We know that Larry Page is an academic at heart with a penchant for relevance. His inspirations are coming from library science as well as other hipper AI methodologies. Throughout my entire frisking career, the one concept that's always held true to the core was *bibliometrics*, otherwise known as citation analysis.

Think of bibliometrics in practice for SEOs as akin to a research paper for university academics. The central concept for relevant search results is finding what we want along with a sense that it came from a credible source. When you're thinking about who should link back to your site, think about who you'd want a referral from in *real* life. If you want a summer internship at the hottest startup in town, who would you ask? Probably not your tennis coach! You'd be more likely to ask your science or math teacher(s), because it would be more credible.

Achieving relevance—not the dissection of AI concepts—is our guiding principle. Be useful to and thoughtful about your site visitors and you'll succeed. Search algorithm obsession is not the safest place for an SEO to stay mentally. Living in fear of updates to core rankings means *you're doing it wrong*. Anticipating penalization is not an effective means to avoid it. Virtually every SEO has an algorithm update horror story to tell.

One of Google's algorithm updates was coined *Panda* back in 2011. The update sought to downgrade poor quality content from search results. Panda hurt many warehouse-style sites that were basically crude content and linking farms. Some SEOs cried for days, because they could no longer "power it out." Things took a more complicated turn. Updates were then made to Panda periodically and sporadically thereafter. Panda's formal inclusion in the core algorithm (*http://selnd.com/2mcoxTl*) was announced in January 2016.

Rolling Panda into the core signifies the move towards AI and machine learning for the engine's algorithm itself. So meta! Once an update gets rolled into the core algorithm, it then runs by itself and no longer needs any testing or maintenance.

As the old adage says, paranoia will destroy ya. Don't worry about each tiny update. Look at the groupings; otherwise, you're chasing ghosts. Google has publicly urged webmasters and SEOs to not fixate on each individual component of their core algorithm:

> For a user or even a webmaster it should not matter at all which components live where, it's really irrelevant, and that's why I think people should focus on these "interesting" things less.
>
> —Gary Illyes, Google webmaster trends analyst

## Practice Areas of SEO

What does a search optimization program cover? It's necessary to understand what marketing activities relate to SEO. When the search program doesn't reach into the right areas, the program can be rendered ineffective. An SEO unable to directly influence changes made to the website runs a powerless program. Web development is one of the most important pieces of an SEO program. Users will no longer tolerate slow performance in a website.

It's imperative to first examine which search engine optimization areas will need oversight for an SEO program. There are two audiences that search must consider: carbon-based life forms and the artificially intelligent computational silicon ones. When building or maintaining a search program, it's paramount that all of the pieces of marketing work together like clockwork. There is no simple tweak that conquers all for SEO—no all-in-one solution. All the pieces have to work together in concert.

Countless people have asked me different versions of the same question over the years: *what is the silver SEO bullet?* They want some hot tip that they think is a secret to search success. Depending on my mood, I'll answer with something like, "Be interesting" or "Get faster." One cannot simply unsheath magical daggers to slay search engine dragons. There is no single tip I could give that would tangibly help a person further their search domination. No matter how much fun I have with my responses, people often seem disappointed (if they do not chuckle). There is never one single piece of *hot goss* (i.e., some big secret) that's going to take you over the top without meaningful context or insights. SEO will never be a one-size-fits-all exercise.

Analytics and data modeling are what initially drove me to become an SEO. I noticed that when I made changes to my sites (and tracked them), sometimes traffic would increase. Slowly, I tinkered and figured out what resulted in more traffic. Relevance met with analytics instrumentation is the winningest combination. An SEO professional without analytics is a blind one; analytics are the key for measuring which tactics work and which do not.

There's essentially no argument that can be made to discount analytics as a core part of SEO programs. Perhaps it could be argued that mobile app installs or a mobile application's analytics wouldn't fall under SEO, but they still fall under app store optimization (ASO). App store optimization for mobile applications is a colossal industry. Much of mobile optimization relied on paid search in the beginning, but not anymore. ASO is the cool Canadian cousin of SEO and the two can work together in terms of linking. Deep linking from within mobile apps can bring much needed oomph to mobile search efforts. When I say "oomph" I mean credibility in the eyes of the engines. Sentiment is an increasingly interesting factor for search (and social media). As machine learning evolves, along with hardware, detecting sentiment should gain importance over time.

Content and outbound communications are crucial for engaging humans and their counterparts (i.e, robots, crawlers and spiders). Compelling content that excites people fosters a site's search dominance far more than thin corporate advertising coupled with stock imagery. Corporate communications like public relations, social media, and email also fall under the SEO umbrella. Keywords and phrases used in communications should involve thoughtful research from the outset. Planning keyword targets and goals *together* is of the utmost importance for all outbound communications.

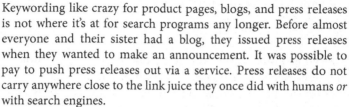

### Penny-Wise, Search-Foolish

Keywording like crazy for product pages, blogs, and press releases is not where it's at for search programs any longer. Before almost everyone and their sister had a blog, they issued press releases when they wanted to make an announcement. It was possible to pay to push press releases out via a service. Press releases do not carry anywhere close to the link juice they once did with humans *or* with search engines.

There are many sites and services that offer to help place press releases for SEO and public relations gains. Anything *you* can pay for, *everyone* else in the world can pay for, too. How is that a key advantage? Be cautious of sites offering "exclusive placement" for pay. "Limited time" and exclusive promotional offers rarely are exclusive in reality. It's important to make the user feel like they're crossing a *velvet rope*, gaining entrance to the hottest nightclub in town. Bouncers sit outside the club (not inside it) to give an illusion of prestige. Just like a nightclub, calls to action should feel exclusive. Make your user feel special—not like any random stranger off of the street can just walk in.

## Email

There are many facets of outbound communications to consider. Optimizing content can definitely *help* search programs, but it cannot lead them. An unexpected example of outbound communique for helping search is email. Yes, email. You are probably wondering how email relates to SEO. Email is a gray-haired business tool and remains the ultimate survivor of the old-school marketing tool chest. The most aged of marketing methods is word of mouth, such as referrals from happy customers. Collect the emails of your advocates and do not abuse their trust. Attaining effortless yet enthusiastic referrals is the key to scalable growth; email is the uncool minivan taking you there. Your net promoters are those customers who are engaged with your site, so emailing them is a slam dunk.

Umpteen tools purport to someday replace email (or make it more extreme) and they have come and gone. Email marketing remains useful because it drives traffic and revenue effectively for a very low cost. Email marketing also cross-pollinates SEO by boosting engagement with and visibility of a site's content. A well-curated email list can drive revenue masterfully. For example, if you allow public blog comments, a targeted email to your net promoters can yield a significant number of page views, shares, and user-generated content.

Email updates or newsletters with substantive information can also be placed on the site for content purposes. If site visitors devotedly pour over the information they see in an email, they'll probably revel in it on a website. Sites could potentially see rankings affected by email issues like excessive unsubscribe or junk mail flags. We could someday see email used as an official ranking signal. Swell!

## Social media

Now that we've had our lovefest on the virtues of email, let's look at the new kid on the search block—social media and social bookmarking. There's a sharp dividing line between SEOs who believe social doesn't count toward search relevance and those who do. The main argument for detractors of social SEO say that major search engines do not officially recognize it as a direct ranking factor. This is a misleading line of logic. Search engines also don't espouse that the sky is blue. The major engines do not announce everything they consider when calculating results. The cloak-and-dagger element makes it a little more fun. *No* search engine will ever release details of the inner workings of core super-warrior stuff. Why would the fact that engines don't officially acknowledge social media matter?

Social sends traffic and often gets indexed, so—recognized or not—it directly impacts search. It's a classic feedback loop. I'm a go-getter type who comes from a place of yes when trying new things, so I say yes—let's assume it matters! Social media also brings traffic to a website. What brings the traffic brings the thunder, then the rain. Social is an ever-changing element that delivers relevant experiences. We should expect to see search *within* social start to matter more and more. After many years of studying numerous companies' analytics, I have noticed that when social traffic goes up, organic search generally does as well.

Healthy social traffic certainly doesn't hurt SEO efforts. Social media and social aggregators provide a lightning-fast number of natural back links and traffic. Social media services like Twitter and LinkedIn are currently being indexed by most major search engines. Aggregators like Reddit or Product Hunt will blow your traffic numbers out of the water.

There are umpteen factors colliding in the search results you see, including location, device used, sessions you're logged into, if you are walking while searching on a phone or standing still, and so on. Location is one of the most financially valuable metrics used in mobile advertising. Therefore, location-based marketers should embrace social for mobile on paid and organic fronts.

Thought and care should be given to social when formulating a search-program strategy. For example, right now tweets are getting indexed. Search Google, and you will see tweets in the results. Next year, they could formally partner or do a revenue share if they're not secretly doing it already. If I'm your SEO, then I'm going to consider anything that builds my relevance, territory, and magnification of signals. If you add all the data together, it's hard to ignore social's impact on traffic.

### Web development

Some organizations choose to silo web development from marketing, which is a mistake. It is hard to imagine success in organic search without the ability to implement changes quickly on the homepage. An SEO without access or authority to change what's on the company homepage is doubtlessly hampered. The person who has the responsibility of managing the homepage's search performance should also have some level of influence. If people have no power to affect change, then they cannot do their jobs. Failing that the data can do the talking. If the mobile version of the site differs from desktop for some reason, this should also be included under SEO. Website development efficiency and efficacy have become key elements of search performance with the advent of mobile's popularity.

Ideally, the search practitioner should lead or get involved in the user interface and experience of a website. The analytics instrumentation becomes especially important when it comes to assessing performance. In this context, *instrumentation* means the integrity and veracity of the analytics setup. If the analytics tools were deployed prior to an SEO's arrival, then he or she must find reasonable evidence that lead-tracking sources are properly capturing.

**You May Be Wondering, Does SEO Cover All Aspects of Internet Marketing?**

While an SEO practitioner doesn't necessarily have to directly manage all of the previously mentioned practice areas, it's ideal for communication to be happening between these entities. An SEO who doesn't know about upcoming site updates won't know when to do their jobs. Strong communication between departments means the team will catch things like whether or not the tracking scripts are still intact after a site update, and whether or not they need to make the annotations in analytics for notable events. Annotation-worthy examples include a product or campaign launch, a new speed fix, etc.

The most successful SEO programs I've built contained the right combination of *both the head and the heart*. Content is the heart of SEO. Content must convey sentiment for people to be able to empathize and connect with it. Analytics, website optimization, and the more technical aspects are governed by the cogent side— the head.

## Types of SEO Practitioners

I have identified at least four distinct types of SEOs over the past decade. It is likely that most people will be a blend of types, because everyone's experiences are unique. People often teach themselves SEO out in the field, because most start their careers as something else. In my case, I started as a web developer and migrated to SEO through my love of analytics. There are only a few places that offer formal SEO training like O'Reilly (*https://www.oreilly.com/*), Bruce Clay (*http://www.bruce clay.com/*), or Udemy.com (*https://www.udemy.com/*). It's more common to "go rogue," as they say.

## Data analytics

Understanding large sets of data and knowing how to parse them is an art, but it calls for an analytical mindset. The analytics SEO is a former data scientist, quant, statistician, scientist, analyst, or someone who is very advanced with their analysis and knowledge of tools. These SEOs operate mostly from the head—not the creative realm (which they find annoying). They are the person who owns the task of correlating data, building dashboards, and ensuring that reports can be trusted. Sometimes a pay-per-click (PPC) person can become a data-focused SEO as well, making them a hybrid. The most important function of this type of SEO is that they learn from the past and measure the future.

## Technical

Technical SEOs are typically former web developers, web designers, or software engineers who get into the SEO field after gaining the desire to be involved in what's on the front of the page, not just what's behind it. The technical SEO will always start with what I like to call the block-and-tackle elements: W3C compliance, data capture, and all the key technical elements that could cause issues with site growth. Also expect some on-page SEO, too, as UI and UX discussion falls within their realm. The limit to working with this type of SEO is that development resources are often the most expensive to a marketing department. The technical SEO will require more than administrative access to WordPress to thrive and enact meaningful changes.

## Content and communications

Content SEOs tend to be less technically driven because their focus is almost all on-page. They have a heavy target goal of gaining website traffic via social generation and gaining links at the core of their programs. This type of SEO is often your content *bartender*, constantly experimenting with the finest in artisanal small-batch traffic sources. The content SEO tends to come from previous careers in writing, branding, corporate communications, public relations, or social media. Content SEOs are hooked on finding new sources of traffic for their sites, and pursue link building programs and new platforms aggressively. They also tend to be fun at parties.

## General/novice

I have inherited a great deal of projects from general/novice SEOs. They tend to be someone who tries their hand at some SEO plugins in WordPress and experiences success because they have a willingness to learn. These types of SEOs are less experienced so they tend to have the one-size-fits-all approach, initially picked up from things like cheesy all-in-one SEO tools. Then they learn.

We all started out as novices at one point; if you encounter one, be encouraging! If your budget only allows for one person to run marketing, the novice will generally work the hardest and cover the most ground. Recognize and accept their learning curve and build some education into the job so they can fly.

## Agency versus in-house SEO practitioners

Regardless of the type of SEO needed, many companies struggle with whether or not to hire an in-house SEO or go with an outsourced agency or consultant. My bias is significant as an agency operator, but I'll still say that agency SEOs have the power to stay up-to-date on trends in a way that in-house ones do not. House SEOs sometimes have the ability to see large amounts of data sets if they are in publishing or ecommerce properties (or with PPC to also manage).

Agency SEOs have an edge because they have access to independent sets of data that span across different industries. If the agency shares some commonalities with the client's industry or geography, this can lead to unique insights. Viewing multiple sets of industry data with similar themes like "business to business" *plus* "technology industry" allows for insights into parallel universes, such as potential upcoming algorithm dips and bumps.

One compelling reason to hire in-house for SEO is when the institution is largely dependent on SEO as a primary means of income. In this case, it's smart to keep the resources, history, and knowledge in-house. If resources are sufficient, it's ideal to have both in-house and agency search marketers collaborating together. Differing perspectives can benefit an SEO program, because more ideas mean more experiments to run.

For a search program to be successful, it must also be specific and clear. Each project should be treated like a special snowflake. If you are aware of your institution's resources and strengths, you'll know which type of practitioner to work with. For example, imagine that you have a technical product in the B2B (business to business) space. You're working with a frontend web development team, but they are all mostly working on making the product and therefore loathe website change requests. So rather than asking the website developers to enact an SEO program, you're better off turning to the technical SEO practitioner, because they'll work efficiently with a developer to quickly enact code changes. Some technical SEOs even know which tools to run on a CMS for sweet results.

## SEO Versus Growth Hacking

*SEO* is the group of practices for optimizing and increasing presence in search engines. *Growth hacking* is the practice of deploying a search program that is hyper-focused on growth, which involves deploying any tactics needed to reach scalable growth. There is a heavy crossover between the two disciplines, but the goals are the same: to increase visibility and prominence for the website or app being promoted.

Let's start with definitions. The timeframes tend to vary for experimentation purposes, but SEO is to longevity as growth hacking is to brevity. Growth is typically measured in units such as traffic, new user signups, revenue, and final sales transactions. SEO covers legions of practice areas, so it's common for practitioners to get pulled into other areas, potentially diluting their focus on search.

It is believed by many in the industry that Sean Ellis coined the term *growth hacker* in 2010.

> A Growth Hacker is a person whose true north is growth. Everything they do is scrutinized by its potential impact on scalable growth. Is positioning important? Only if a case can be made that it is important for driving sustainable growth.
>
> —Sean Ellis (*http://whatis.techtarget.com/definition/growth-hacker*), growth-hacking godfather

In Silicon Valley everyone wants to find the sharp path to growth, otherwise commonly known as *the hockey stick*. The "stick" equates to the line depicting sharp growth increases, often physically shown in analytics. To possess the hockey stick is to hold the key to scalable growth and make it to the big leagues, or sometimes the zeitgeist.

Growth hacking's significance as a movement signals the entrance of developers and assorted techie hybrids into traditional marketing roles. In Silicon Valley many start-ups are experiencing the influx of developers and more technical folks into marketing leadership roles. It's very common for the CTO or COO to also be the CMO in the beginning; I think that's A-OK because sometimes very fun things can happen.

The two types of marketing seem like peas in a pod from the outset. SEO has a somewhat notorious reputation with a fair amount of developers. Some respect it and some see it as folklore. Some cannot understand how anyone could manipulate search without having direct access to the search algorithms; they believe SEO is not real. There are conspiracy theorists for almost everything, I guess. On the contrary, growth hacking seems to be more of an acceptable practice to many developers I've spoken to. CMO's eyes light up when they hear *growth hacking*; it feels new and chi-chi.

The biggest difference between the two approaches is the level of formality and experimentation. There's no actual "hacking" happening in growth hacking, unless the practitioners are donning their black hats off into the sunset. Many growth hackers started out as developers. Perhaps the *hacking* in this case means parting from traditional marketing realms and roles. Growth hackers extend beyond marketing into product development, because user retention is a key goal. Some of the most historic cases of explosive growth hacking success involved input into product development as well.

*Hacking* in the classic sense involves exploiting vulnerabilities in a system or network. A growth hacking "hack" in practice would then look disreputable. For example, a hack practice could be paying money for cheap traffic and then claiming it's organic or from another less dubious traffic source. Cheaters tend to assume others will be taking shortcuts as well, so they're betting their client doesn't know the difference between types of traffic or how to look it up themselves.

Functionally, growth hacking means exploiting search engine weakness not *human* weakness—but philosophically it means identifying advancement and revenue opportunities quickly. SEO and growth hacking are essentially the same in my mind, but one feels a bit more *eXtreme to the maxxx.*

## How Do Successful SEOs Allocate Their Time?

SEOs should dedicate their time to four major areas: reading, data analysis, testing new tools, and monitoring/automation. Without a commitment to master the four key areas, an SEO is doomed to fall behind eventually. Continuous learning is the most paramount activity for an SEO.

Every morning starts with reading news, blogs (sometimes the comments too), chatter on social, and industry journals as well as outsider pieces. Though it's sometimes hard to keep up with everything if you're also the practitioner, it's important to stay well-read on the topics that matter to your specific company or industry. Topics should definitely include search trends as well as top companies in the search industry, such as LinkedIn, Facebook, and Twitter.

Research can also be automated in many ways. Beyond search-triggered alerts, there are also social alerts and automated recipe alerts. Tools like IFTTT (*http://www.ifttt.com*) are a great way to aggregate content about a given topic on infinite mediums. I have some Twitter accounts that only exist to automatically feed me the information I want on a certain topic. The most critical thing to automate is competitor research. One should always keep an eye on those who want to take your spot.

Data analysis is another critical role for the SEO in charge of a search program. Understanding at all times what is happening with your site from both a webmaster and statistician's viewpoint will only reap benefits. Data must be sliced and diced from different dimensions to show trends. Six months of data or more are typically needed to make significant organic revelations. In many cases, paid search is much faster for testing user flow or usability.

There's a difference between knowing your data and suffering from "analysis paralysis" (i.e., the obsession with data to the point it is ineffective to attain positive business results). There's another strong case for automation with data analysis. Building dashboards in Google Analytics takes minutes and they can then be emailed daily or weekly depending on the demand.

Aside from dashboards, it's good to go into any analytics tool with a rough idea of what you want to learn or prove. Staring at overviews of data for the sake of it isn't a good use of time. My terminology (borrowed from Sherlock Holmes) is that I like to step inside my *mind palace*.

Here's what that means in practice:

1. Make some assertions based on gut instinct and experience (i.e., for selling to businesses, LinkedIn is our top social lead converting source).
2. Keep an open mind as you sift through different data sources and views.
3. Study the data impartially to see what can be proven or disproved with confidence.

Testing out new tools is one of my favorite things to do. So many tools promise one-size-fits-all analytics insights; some purport to tell the future with predictive analytics. Be leery of tools that produce junky code that loads slowly. Watch out for tools that attempt to capriciously control your future, like how some CDN's hijack one's link-juice via overzealous subdomains.

The best SEO colleagues I have worked with and studied under all have a handful of tools in their arsenal. It's usually a blend of search engine hosted tools, third-party testing tools, and automation tools. We'll go into more detail on specific tools in Chapter 4, but I cannot stress enough that there's no one-size-fits-all tool on the market right now (although many claim that).

From news aggregation to data segmentation, many essential functions of the SEO brain-trust call for automation. To truly stay on top of everything, you will need the help of bots. Do not fear bots—they are your allies (most of the time). The SEO's audience is generally half-human and half-bot/crawler/spider. So it makes sense to implore help from some of your cool bot friends.

**Movement Is Not Momentum**

One of the biggest SEO issues I see many companies wrestle with is conflating movement with momentum. Movement means making a bunch of changes to a site based on hunches. Momentum means running programs with discipline and consistent growth month after month. There is no silver SEO bullet. The strongest SEO programs are organized machines running in concert with the marketing and development departments.

The reason SEO caught my interest so many years ago is that, fundamentally speaking, search is a garden that's always growing. The search field of practice introduces analytical thinking with creativity and a dash of data. Art meets science. You can write funny tweets and strategically unleash them at *just* the right moment and then watch your traffic soar. If you do not fight for your turf online, then other people will.

# Standing Apart

To stand apart and get page views, you have to be copiously unafraid to try unfamiliar things. With each new search project, an SEO should shed his or her previous biases and, even more importantly, successes. I liken search marketers to ancient resting ram sharks who had to constantly move throughout the ocean to survive.

Every SEO program should be unique; each target audience has a place, too. There are demographics that convert better on Bing, like older males living in the Midwest. DuckDuckGo (DDG) has also gained steam in recent years. The indie hip browser DDG started in 2008 to a slew of skepticism and proved everyone wrong with 500% year over year growth.

DDG's key differentiator in the market is security; they claim to not collect personal information like the other search engines do. In a post-Snowden world, people are far more concerned about privacy online than ever before. DDG also allows the user to heavily customize their own user experience. We should expect to see more and more segmentation and new search engines being born as niche audiences form and methods of input expand.

A good SEO plan starts out with an audit; begin by verifying all the details and putting together the full picture of the landscape.

---

## The Future Is Near

Old SEO practices meant a huge emphasis on keywords. Because of the popularity of mobile and speech-to-text, the focus for a program should be more on natural language. Don't get hyper-focused on particular short-form keyword searches unless you're convinced by overwhelming data that it is generating revenue. The field of

---

search engine optimization was once focused on one major goal: harvesting intent from search.

The emerging practices of search marketing involve more than capturing what people are already looking for because there are many new places for sites to get found. Acquisition strategies within programs now often include *generating* intention as well as capturing it.

We know that SEO will continue to evolve through different devices and platforms. I believe that search will be powered by voice on mobile more and more in the next few years. The inputs and outputs are changing; the data layers are being mapped but cannot yet be understood or correlated. We're not just in text-land anymore, Dorothy. Search never truly was a text-only game—input methods like images, voice, and video content can be optimized for search. The number of people utilizing a smartphone with a voice search function has steadily increased since the introduction of Siri. Voice is consistently overtaking its own numbers, month after month.

Smartphone users have Cortana, Google Now, and Siri to help them while they are on the go. Digital assistants have begun offering a safer way to look up information while driving or multitasking.

What you will get from reading this book:

- How to perform keyword research and spot search trends
- Ways to think about the discipline of mindsets of SEO
- A working knowledge of how to run a campaign for traffic generation with analytics measurement
- Mobile and platform-agnostic strategies for search growth
- How to demonstrate value from organic marketing efforts
- The ability to ensure the fiscal integrity of a site
- The sweetest way to run and report on an organic search program

If you stay disciplined about pursuing your search education, you will rise to become an SEO superstar. Let's do this!

# CHAPTER 2

# The SEO Mindset

SEO and growth hacking share a common root—the mutual desire to grow a site's traffic—and both disciplines fall under the umbrella of search marketing. In this chapter we're setting the stage for how to get creatively motivated to increase traffic and learn how to kite trends. Kiting internet trends is one of the most exciting things search marketers do. Simply having an awareness of opportunities allows a search marketer to expand his or her audience. Getting screen time from visitors to a site depends on how well you know who you're trying to target and how much you can tickle them. Competition is cutthroat and new platforms are constantly emerging.

## Getting into the Growth Zone

So you want to be a growth hacker. You've come to the right place. How does one step into this mercurial, money-making mindset? The answer lies in the right combination of experimentation, data analysis, persistence, and moxie. If another site is dominating your search landscape, the right research can help you understand why. Much can be learned from studying what is already out there on the web. I learned how to grow my traffic strategies by learning to dissect those that were in front of me.

Accept from day one that nothing will ever be handed to you; the engines do nobody any favors. The results will always favor the user—and they should. My point is that the arsenal of traffic strategies you secure are *yours to build*.

As Warren Buffet put it so succinctly: "Never invest in anything you don't understand." Make no mistake, SEO is an investment.

When marketing a site, your philosophy colors everything. Are you positive about the site? Are you excited? If not, get that way! Begin the journey by *stepping into* the discovery mindset. It's not always an easy thing to grow a website, but your perceived reality will determine your approach to building growth. Maintain a keen eye toward new potential search moves to be made and partnerships forged. I have always believed that to help a site's traffic grow *full tilt* requires imaginative exploration coupled with scientific discipline. Top growth marketers masterfully combine their creative endeavors with data capture and analysis. Curiosity with a hint of skepticism should be exercised when determining potential areas for growth online. The key to long-term growth is testing and then adjusting course correctly. To test should mean you are going to learn; therefore, *learning* from tests means *integration,* which in turn creates growth patterns.

There's an expression people use in business: don't boil the ocean. To *go for it* and go for everything in terms of search sometimes means that you're likely to accomplish nothing. Decisions must be made at the outset of any project. Which role should the search practitioner play? Maybe the project reeks of data drama (i.e., are we seeing too much dark traffic in analytics?). Are the load times painfully lackadaisical on mobile due to large video assets and inadequate hosting packages? The most important targeting decision is to figure out who the target actually is. Be open to targets you wouldn't normally consider. I've seen businesses delighted by the fact that their income derives from happy customers, but care must be given to *finding* that information. Once the search targets are properly identified, all other decisions will naturally flow from that.

The content and physical piece of the puzzle is referred to as *on-page SEO.* Always think about the user and why they are visiting your site in the first place. What are they getting in exchange for coming to your site? Is it what they want or is it what you want? Data analysis works in concert with the creative elements to aid the practitioner in navigating the decision-making process.

Growth marketing as a profession cannot and should not be scalable, for it cannot be applied generically. Universal concepts and methods of testing can be applied to most sites, but each case is unique. Take running developer tool audits or diagnostic tools. They will generally return some result that needs attention. The key to growth is to set yourself up for it by having clean code, optimized pages for usability, and generally decent information for the user to consume. The balance of art and science that's called for varies for every new project. Sometimes the first step is *not* to do the right things (better), but rather to stop doing the *wrong* things.

In summary, it is not a winning idea to think about SEO in terms of being a one-hit wonder. A search champion's mindset is not to think, "We did that one thing and so —yeah, cool—we did SEO." A one-dimensional approach seeking to game the search engines or a platform is not a long-term strategy.

SEOs should operate in a similar style to David Bowie; with his tireless evolution and collaboration between channels, habitual artistry, and innovation, he managed to stay relevant for decades while maintaining his creative integrity. A superior strategy over trickery is to put the time in, study, experiment, and *always* measure everything.

You don't learn to walk by following rules. You learn by doing, and by falling over.

—Richard Branson (*https://www.virgin.com/richard-branson/you-learn-by-doing-and-by-falling-over*), business magnate, investor, and philanthropist

Some of the best ideas for growth I've ever had have come from mucking around with my own stuff or someone else's. It's like riffing to your favorite jam on the radio and creating your own silly songs. Experimenting requires thoughtful tinkering. One of my tried and true tinker methods is to explore sites built by intriguing companies. I will often examine pages thoroughly to learn what they're doing on their homepages, blogs, shopping carts, etc.

Sometimes I'll go so far as to fill out their web forms to see how they market themselves effectively through email. I like to see what it's like to hop in their funnel: how is the experience? Is it exciting? Is there ample feedback? Is it fun? Be honest with yourself; if you spare their feelings, remember that the general public won't always be as kind.

## Creating Fake Email Boxes for Fun and Profit

When you test a form, you're really performing competitive analysis. In order to keep track of each form and any responses, the scientific approach is to use separate email aliases for each client (or even each test or group of tests).

In general, it's a good idea to create an email alias specific to the form so you can test how virtuous it is. Did they ask for my phone number, claim to not use it but do so anyway? Does the company follow the CAN-SPAM Act of 2003 (*https://en.wikipedia.org/wiki/CAN-SPAM_Act_of_2003*)?

It may not seem like a big deal at first, but once you begin testing different things you will thank yourself (or hopefully me) later. Give a hoot, don't pollute your inbox.

Many popular web email sites (like Gmail) will let you modify your address to create an alias on the fly. Let's say your email address is *foo@email.com*; in many instances you can create *foo+test1@barrrr.com*. If you're unsure, just test it. :)

### Don't Forget to Check the Favicon

One of the most interesting elements I like to check on a site is the favicon. Web legend has it that the word is a blend of "favorite" and "icon." The favicon is a tiny 16×16 file containing an icon that appears in the browser's bar next to the title of the site (Figure 2-1). Originally intended to help bookmarking and user experience, its presence is one of many clues for how "together" a site is behind the scenes.

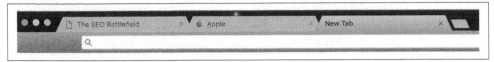

*Figure 2-1. Apple is a solid example. Look how cool it is to have a favicon!*

Where you'll need to cruise for ideas is dependent on what you're working on. Apple is an interesting case to look at for SEO as they have never really "done" a blog in the classic sense, so their site is not necessarily a good example for content layouts. If you are enhancing a shopping cart for better click-through rates (CTR), it would make sense to study Apple's cart because they sell millions of dollars in products online every month (*http://bit.ly/2mfnN18*), despite speculation of a decline in recent years. If you are creating a blog with heavy imagery, then it's better to study sites like Lyft (*https://www.lyft.com*), Fubiz (*http://www.fubiz.net*), or Quartz (*http://qz.com*) because they have delightful layouts. Without an inviting layout, your content has less of a chance to be seen. Users are especially fickle when it comes to mobile layout and design, because the time on site is less than desktop.

Even if the goals of a site do not line up with what you're working on, ideas can be gained by studying who's on top. Make sure to review the sites on desktop, mobile, tablet, TV, etc. and note the subtle differences. Responsive or not, the experiences should be crisp for each user on every platform. Websites have had browser sniffing and redirecting capabilities for the better part of a decade.

Just like flipping through fashion magazines for wardrobe ideas, perusing sites that are *crushing it* helps an SEO to gain a sense of "what's in" this season. By studying strategies of others with mad traffic, you start to get the sense for what users are responding to and how usability changes over time.

---

## How Big Are You?

There are a number of factors or signals of growth other than what you can see in search results. Raw traffic is generally a rough estimate of success to some degree. If you're curious how dominant a site is in the engines, it's easy to look up their estimates on traffic measurement sites like Quantcast (*https://www.quantcast.com*).

Many people like to research using quality indicators like PageRank or Moz rank (*https://moz.com/learn/seo/mozrank*) to find out how much authority a page has. In March 2016, Google confirmed (*http://selnd.com/2muFD0O*) that it would no longer allow toolbars to use the PageRank checker in the browser, so a host of clones will likely pop up.

---

When you've spent a great deal of time working on a site or managing a site, it's really easy to be blind to the little things. Competitive research is where you have the opportunity to tighten things up. There is invaluable information to be gained by researching sites in terms of physicality (i.e., source, layout, forms, etc.). You can see who registered a website, where they're hosting it, and how many site managers they have. Check the hosting and registration information of any website by doing a Whois (*http://whois.domaintools.com*) lookup. If a site is using fancier services like Rackspace or Akamai, then they're probably serious about their performance. Are they cloaking their information? That's also information to keep under your hat. If they're cloaking information, are they who they say they are? Is this project a competitor trying to look like someone else? Information gathering is so crucial in research; gather it and then tabulate it. The trends will start to appear!

Let's say you hear about a contest being run by a cool new tech company. The creatives on the website are amazing, but you don't know much about how it was put together.

Here are a few example steps to break that web page down:

1. Maybe an agency put it together soup to nuts? Look up the Whois registry information. You can actually check that by seeing who registered the domain.
2. Check the source for any and all tools used. Is tracking deployed? What pixels or rich snippets are there? Sometimes comments in the source can be telling.
3. Click on any interactive elements and then Ctrl-click to see them isolated in a new window. From there, you can tell if they're a gif or a script, etc.
4. Enter the contest! Hey, maybe you'll win—either way, you can see what the emails look like. Enter their marketing machine. Trends change, but maybe their emails are on point and inspire you to revisit your own strategy.

# Gaining Authenticity

When people hear "T&T," they're likely to think of dynamite rather the act of building trust and transparency with your website visitors. Conversions come purely from building trust with the people sitting on the other end of the inter-tubes. Why does trust matter so much? Because *nobody* wants to get hoodwinked. Most people have developed a sense for when they might get deceived online, especially during a financial transaction. As search marketers, we must first gain trust to get a web form fill or conversion. Conversions happen only when a visitor's comfort levels in trust and transparency are met.

There are two main philosophical buckets of practices for SEO: black hat and white hat. The term *black hat* originates from before search was a *thing*, with old cowboy western movies. The color of the cowboy's hat denoted if it was a good or a bad guy riding toward the protagonist. The hero, often in white, was painted as the good character, the one who unties the girl from the train tracks, etc. Zorro (*https://en.wikipedia.org/wiki/Zorro*) is the only exception to this; he wore black. He operated as an outlaw, yet wearing black probably made him seem cooler to the audience—an unexpected hero who fought for regular people.

Search engine optimization is not like the movies, but philosophically an SEO always needs to don the white hat. The difference between the two types of methods is *deception*. I think of black versus white hat in terms of *night versus day*. People who embark on black hat SEO tactics have to operate in the darkness (to some extent). They lurk in the shadows since it's atypical to see anyone declare their evil machinations to the world. Users do not get what they came for; they fill out information under false pretenses. Further black hat examples could be misleading link bait from ads for poorly targeted news articles, clicking on links spawning extra windows, or simply only dealing with robots (in a shady way).

White hat SEOs operate above board, performing work that will benefit their sites long term. They also deliver what they promise to the user as they enter the site. Deception is never the basis of a sound business strategy. Black hat methods include knowingly violating the terms of service for any engine, tool, or platform. Black hat SEOs spend nights scheming and biding time before getting caught, such as using bots to take down competition or just generally being kind of evil (you know who you are).

It's not just the search machines that black hat SEOs can deceive, it's the site visitor. Taking someone's email and spamming them mercilessly without the appropriate unsubscribe links or reselling private information to other sites is also black hat. Violating your first implied agreement with someone does not build trust; it builds bad user experiences, which can, in extreme cases, spill over to social media. This is not good attention.

Only 5% (or less) of top websites are performing at the level where black hat methods reap huge financial rewards, but even then the risks are just as great.

> Integrity is the essence of everything successful.
>
> —R. Buckminster Fuller

Black hat SEO tactics sometimes self-characterize as gray hats, but gray does not fundamentally exist without the presence of black. I've seen many companies wrestle with their preconceived notions of right and wrong, and the ones that use shady tactics seldom win in the end. Doing things to competitors like using advanced knowledge of current search engine penalties from algorithm changes to sink them is an aggressive move by *meanie*-hat SEOs. Building trust means advocating for the site visitor to get what they're promised. Page meta descriptions appear in search results, which means they should *always* match the page's content. People often click away from a site if they do not get what is suggested to them; some SEOs call this "the scent; the essence of truthiness."

Unfortunately, black hat tactics against competitors will sometimes work enough to sink their site temporarily. It's possible to use knowledge of search engines to negatively influence another's ranking. The sinking of others only works until the website's administrator and/or SEO discovers what's happening. There are remedies that a company can take when they encounter bad traffic or other competitor activity. If these things happen to you, it's unfortunate, but you can report violations with terms of service easily for either paid or organic issues to the engines themselves.

Sometimes the type of trust issue you're faced with is related to reputation or branding. Reputation has become a form of currency on the internet. Issues related to reputation are generally one of two things: a site's brand is not appearing where it should in the SERPs or unsavory results appear at the top of a branded query. The approach to solving these problems is to handle with care.

Trust between a potential customer and a company must be present for a potential customer become a customer. Many companies seek to manipulate how they appear, especially if mistakes have been made. Manipulation erodes user trust. Simple things like including the name and picture of the author of a blog or linking to their biography can help establish trust. If you're trying to build credibility, then make the effort to cite the information you're referencing and link out if it makes sense.

Some growth opportunities are too good to be true. While it's tempting to bribe your way into credibility, it's dangerous. Maybe you hear of a hot new service offering pay-for-play content placement or easy reviews in the app store. Deception cuts both ways. Sites that seek payment to assist in building trust should be given thorough examination. Ask for references or get a case study to determine if the service is legitimate. If a vendor cannot tell you specific results they've gotten for other people, they do not warrant your trust.

The most important thing with a trust or brand problem is to never try to squash the truth. The internet gets the most angry when it feels lied to. People will often forgive mistakes made by companies, but they will not forgive insincerity. Nobody can be the internet's police. We can only try to direct where things go as traffic cops (pun intended).

Clients have often asked me if it's OK to ask for reviews from customers. My philosophy is to ask the customer two questions: are you active on Yelp (or review site in question)? If so, would you feel comfortable giving us a review online? Then it's good to also explain why their review is helpful to you, such as that you are new and need to establish your business online or whatever the real reason is. If the person says no, they have not done any reviews, then do not push for them to leave one.

It's super tempting to right (perceived) wrongs online. Deleting Facebook comments or manipulating your reviews will only make life worse. If the issues in the reviews are real, then deal with them. It can take time, but fixing problems at the root level will allow your online reputation to repair much faster. There's never any reason to buy or pay for reviews. It's far superior for outsiders to leave reviews (even if they're bad), but never the CEO. Employees should not be writing reviews, ever. It's fairly easy to spot an online review written by an employee or owner of a company.

### How to Spot a Fake Review or Comment

Fake reviews can really hurt a company, especially when they are bad. The following are a few tips to help spot fake reviews online:

- Uses stock photos or still uses the service's default images as avatars
- Use of a company logo or well-known celebrity as the avatar
- Extensively long and overly explanatory, especially containing non sequiturs
- Overly friendly or overly angry
- Overly vague reviews
- Nonsensical praise that nobody would say in real life or natural language
- Redundant text or repeated phrases
- The reviewer has not reviewed anything else, ever
- Many reviews submitted in a small period of time
- What they're saying simply sounds too good to be true

Consider also that bots can take hold in the form of scripts. Weirdly repeated phrasings are typically the sign of a spam bot.

# A Day in the Life

The path to growth is paved with bounteous experimental activities. This section seeks to explore the daily routine in the mindset of a growth marketer. Growth hackers by definition cannot stay still in their routines, because "still" is not a valid state of being. Ambitions for the growth hacker are endless. Learning is the most important element to having and maintaining a strong growth mindset. Always stay open to learning what informational analysis reveals and what's happening all around the search ecosphere of the industries you target.

SEOs have to perpetually learn new things. I read about an hour or two every day and watch news in the morning. I listen to podcasts about all sorts of weird topics from survivalist stuff to pure nerd comedy. I also track senseless internet holidays like Geek Pride Day, Towel Day, National Paper Airplane Day, and the always-Twitter-trending National Donut Day. My typical reading consists of various social media sites, blogs, search industry journals, *The New York Times*, *Wall Street Journal*, and various nationally prominent technology and business news sites. Then there's the aggregators, sites such as Reddit, where the line between work and gluttony starts to blur.

On social media, it's beneficial to follow contrasting people, such as fellow top-notch SEOs, online influencers, industry analysts, and journalists in discrete categories. The majority of learning can be done online, but some should be done in real life. It's fairly straightforward to find local Meetups (*http://www.meetup.com*), seminars, and conferences covering the SEO topic areas you will want to start following such as site speed optimization, content marketing, or user experience design. Most cities in the US have events or groups that get together on any variety of fun topics and purposes. Fortunately for me, I've had a few top-notch mentors over the years and their benefits cannot be disputed. It's a winning formula to always have at least one mentor, but also *mentor others* and pay it forward. It's extremely invigorating to help someone gain knowledge about something you take for granted. Learning means excitement for your brain; think of it as a data party. All of this (seemingly) random information we are collecting gives us a broad basis for knowing what's happening across a variety of industries.

Books like *Freakonomics* (William Morrow) and *A Mathematician Reads the Paper* (Basic Books) make data analysis feel so neat and tidy that it's almost cool. The truth is that not everything you read will make your brain's neurons luster like a pearl. The SEO's job often includes needing to make mathematics seem intuitive to their less technical counterparts. Fortunately for us information-hungry types, mobile news sites are now highly optimized for glimmering headlines. Mobile apps like Flipboard (*http://www.flipboard.com*) or CNN make it easy to consume information broadly and quickly. Even newer kids on the block like Snapchat provide a super fun way to consume news.

Continuous targeted learning can help you gain skills for snatching traffic from many mediums, not just the search engines. If my goal is to rank for the search of a new product or service in any given market, then I should also know where the people I'm targeting tend to spend their time online. For example, typically I can predict a fair portion of what will trend on Twitter any given day in any location based on a few things such as ongoing trends for the area, the calendar, the sports that are in season, etc. Predicting the advancing social waves happens when you are looking for traffic from a certain subset of people and have been studying personas.

Like growth hackers, stockbrokers are constantly reading news and finding ways to follow market trends, they share this in common. Brokers deal in currency and stock while SEOs deal in information and data. They follow the same methodology, staying on top of news about select topics to better spot trends. Listening to industry experts and their predictions allows you to look for patterns (i.e., opportunity).

When you read about similar or overlapping areas *every single day*, you start to spot patterns. The best discoveries I've had have come from my own form of pattern recognition, seaming together connective tissues between different information sources. You do not have to become an information or data scientist to keep up on discovering every traffic-gaining source possible. Deriving your income from kiting trends online is not for the faint of heart; commitments must be formed to consume the information surrounding pools of information.

In terms of tracking potential upcoming algorithm updates, it's best to track industry commentary if you do not have access to managing multiple data sets. Industry leaders spend countless hours tracking trends. I enjoy reading and gleaning industry information from sites like Search Engine Journal (*https://www.searchenginejournal.com*) (disclaimer: I sometimes guest write (*https://www.searchenginejournal.com/author/anne-ward*) for them), Search Engine Land (*http://searchengineland.com*), or Moz's blog (*https://moz.com/blog*). For user experience, performance, and web development trends, I really like Smashing Magazine (*https://www.smashingmagazine.com*), DZone (*https://dzone.com*), and Stack Overflow (*http://stackoverflow.com*).

Search optimization is not only reading and research, but also dabbling. The experiments! We borrow from the scientific method in this regard; we form hypotheses and then devise experiments. There's so many good ideas to try out that it's often hard to define the experiment. It's prudent to treat your experiments as campaigns, not as an open-ended freeform chasing of rainbows (or waterfalls). Campaigns have a defined starting and ending point; they are measured and evaluated afterward. Failure is always OK, but ignoring the results and reasons for it are not.

In San Francisco, we're decidedly social media hogs and super crazy about our sports teams and conferences. Anything the Giants, Sharks, A's, 49ers, or Warriors are doing *will* trend on social during those seasons. We also tend to see some fun and classic old-school Twitter trends pop up weekly, like #MotivationMonday and #WomenCrushWednesday (now the leaner #WCW). Tech conferences also seem to trend on Twitter in San Francisco (possibly due to the fact we're the company's home town). In the Bay Area, we often have giant screens near conference stages specifically to display the Twitter feeds from their hashtag to the audience so that people will join in the online conversation. Online conversation means engagement and therefore guaranteed eyeballs for the conference sponsors.

Understanding the market you are living in *and often targeting* gives a keen advantage to also *gain* social traction here. It's simply going to be different in rural areas versus cities like New York, Austin, or Los Angeles. Social mores and folkways are going to vary by region, which makes social media difficult to apply unilaterally with live events. People outside of the tech bubble might even feel that it's super rude to be constantly tweeting about everything that's happening, and online marketers should consider that before choosing a campaign like that. Perhaps for different areas it could be Instagram or Facebook, roughly one post per event. In that case, getting attention may be better sought out by a limited "friends of friends" dark post running on the company's Facebook page that's locked down by location or a Snapchat Geo filter campaign. There's no all-in-one method to fall back on for a social growth hacker; each audience (and platform) should be attended to properly.

Knowledge of an industry is very useful, but so is knowledge of platforms. For example, there's social media, but there's also social bookmarking. *Bookmarking* is the lesser known form of consuming information, and a supportive friend to SEOs; it's also known as *content aggregation*. The largest sites on the internet are either content creation sites or those that cultivate the content of others via user-generated content (UGC) or aggregation.

Classic data aggregation site services are Metafilter and Digg, which are not as popular as more modern services like Scoop.it. People can use a site like Scoop.it to aggregate their own pages of links on certain topics. Done in volume, the index of recommendations start to get some juice. New aggregators and bookmarking sites pop up all the time, and even take new forms like with Pinterest. Pinterest has a steady stream of quality user-generated content (UGC), beautiful UI, and click-bait. When content population starts rolling, so does sharing, and then the traffic is sure to follow.

Platforms or sites that generate quality traffic inexpensively to your site should always get your attention—even if it is a site for lumberjacks and even if it's run by people wearing cat-covered pants. A growth hacker is constantly searching for new ways to grow and collaborate with others in the field. There are some top influencers on the internet that have networks sizable enough to gain mass interest—the Robert Scoble's and Guy Kawasaki's of the world.

Many products have been launched by endorsements. Influencer marketing is on the rise dramatically. Instagram stars can demand thousands of dollars for quick videos featuring a product. The endorsement is most likely to go viral when it is unexpected by the public, like Susan Boyle, a random presidential mention, or the Chewbacca Mom. Live video could soon play a major part in retail endorsements, with the popularity of services like Periscope, Facebook Live, and YouTube.

## Dissect Your SERPs

Apart from analytics, there are other ways to understand any given SEO landscape. Learn the search engine results page (SERP). The best way to know what you're up against is to simply *search it*. Crazy, right?

Look at who is on top, then run reports on what they're linking to and who is linking to them. Are they using SSL? Are they on HTTP/2? Make note of the unique characteristics on-page and in the source. Repetition is key to this type of research. Repetition produces patterns and patterns lead to observations.

When you do the same search queries over time, it will start to become clear what is trending up and down. There are also tools to monitor the rankings, but none can (yet) holistically predict *why* the changes are happening.

# How to Spot Trends

Trend spotters are habitual line steppers. It's almost not a choice; it's a way of thinking. The thrill of the hunt is real! You're going to always have outliers, observations that don't fit into the puzzle. The challenge is to discern the difference between signals and just noise. Seemingly random things become *less so* within the right context. Do not put on your tinfoil hats on yet, because Ello and Peach aren't coming back. Just ask MySpace.

Having a cool website or product is generally not enough to get discovered. Competition for user attention is stiff. Mobile users are spending more and more of their time on fewer platforms. Predicting future viral success online is a craft possessed by a select few and sometimes their success is also based on luck. Finding online growth means unearthing low-cost ways to grow by exploiting an opening somewhere. A less buzzword-y way to describe the practice of trend spotting is *identifying opportunities*.

Monitoring a wide variety of data sets helps an SEO to spot trends and potential algorithm changes. If you're only managing one site, there's another way to spot trends: by measuring specific pages versus rankings via spreadsheet. When changes are made to the pages, be sure to annotate them in analytics. It takes a few weeks at a minimum to measure the page-level way, but with careful monitoring you can determine patterns that emerge. If any campaigns, emails, or paid search are used in conjunction with your specific page monitoring tests, it will throw data off slightly. Depending on the length of time you're monitoring specific page rankings, there could be insights gained from mixed strategies if tracked and also annotated properly.

"Keep learning" sounds like something your high school principal or guidance counselor might have said once, but it is far more serious than some motivational speech. How do soldiers and generals alike prepare for battle? They go the distance, train, research their enemies' capabilities, properly estimate their own capabilities, and deploy all the weapons in their arsenal, from lasers to tanks.

The fact remains that knowledge of one's domain and the tools out there is vital to success. A growth marketer is the most effective when armed with knowledge of emerging information, whether it is about traffic opportunities or the industry or both. Here is a cross-section of trends we might need to know about if we're optimizing in a hyper-competitive local search space for a high-end luxury service that goes door to door:

- Who are the major players in local directory listings?

- Where is the site hosted? NGINX or ELBs? When are updates rolled out?
- When are the next hackathons?
- How are the new Instagram ads converting into traffic?
- Do the new Google publishing rules make it harder to enact Project AMP for large sites?

Monitoring information should include but is not limited to:

- What is the price of fair trade coffee beans?
- What is our biggest competitor doing with their content on Pinterest?
- Who is most likely to buy Twitter?

Trends can take shape in peculiar ways. These questions might seem random, but when forming a picture of a search landscape, the more information used in making decisions, the stronger the program becomes. If the information gathered is going to be useful, you have to think through what the competition is doing, and also what's happening with budget.

---

### Paid Digression

Classic search optimization and growth hacking differ in yet another way. Growth hacking does not exclude paid search because it's typically *guerrilla* and therefore low budget. I have seen growth hacking competitions where small paid campaigns were used for either research or lead generation.

Paid search is still search. An SEO or growth hacker should never ignore the benefits of well-targeted paid search retargeting or paid social in the right situations.

Trends come and go, but money makes traffic happen the fastest. Utilizing paid search or social can address immediate needs for immediate results in the beginning of an organic project. Paid is an expeditious method for a marketer to test keyword viability for conversion.

---

Let's take the example of the growing trend of "wearable computing." Everyone is cuckoo over IoT trends lately, but the levels of knowledge are different. If you want to get ahead for "wearable computing," you've got your work cut out for you! For that particular query, the competition is increasingly steep (see Figure 2-2).

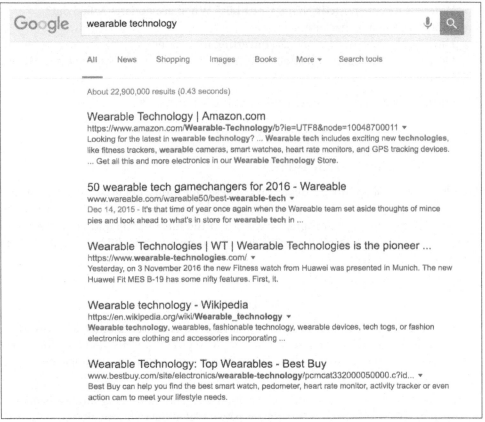

*Figure 2-2. Aye caramba! The results page for "wearable technology" has some heavy hitters.*

There's no real reason to go after this query for a product unless you're running a gigantic ecommerce site selling wearables (like Amazon or Best Buy) or a publication that covers the category (Wikipedia and Wearable). The issue with targeting something too generic is that your competition will be higher for no good reason. Success is harder to reach when targets are too broad. If you're doing SEO in the wearable family of technology, like smart rings or bracelets, why would the above SERP matter to you? That could be a reason to consider for paid search, but only the search *category* of "wearable technology" matters, not page one results.

Watching the trends of the wearable-computing category is helpful because they are the search umbrella (bucket) that jewelry falls under. Sweeping changes in terminology or social interest in the wearable-computing category will trickle down to wearables that are jewelry.

Let's say someone famous on a daytime TV talk show renames "wearables jewelry" to "smart jewelry." The social media explosion that follows is sure to affect search.

> What scares me the most is that both the poker bot and Dropbox started out as distractions. That little voice in my head was telling me where to go, and the whole time I was telling it to shut up so I could get back to work. Sometimes that little voice knows best.
>
> —Drew Houston (*http://bit.ly/2lxeScO*), CEO of Dropbox

It's sometimes hardest to do organic search optimization projects in new category spaces, because the search interest is just not there yet. In these cases, you'll see very few competitors to benchmark against. So what do you do? You research, to the best of your ability, what is related to the new space and place some bets based on trends and search volume. Trust your gut where you see signs of growth.

One rather self-centric example is how I track my own reputation via a search of my online moniker, *Annebot*. As an internet marketing enthusiast, I constantly register for new social sites and professional profiles when I find them. By tracking a singular query over time, it starts to become clearer which services are on the rise. For many years, CNET was in the top five results for a search of my handle; now it's nowhere to be seen.

# Be Data-Agnostic

The struggle is real: it's difficult to avoid bias when reviewing the results of a campaign you've worked hard on. Maybe this campaign was your baby? Maybe your baby is a little less attractive than the others? Perceptions and folklore about a campaign's results within an organization often become *part* of the results (i.e., the executives loved it, so it's a good campaign). Then everyone starts thinking "We are *great*—let's reverse engineer this data and show just how *great* we did." It's natural to be influenced by feedback, but growth marketers have many, many ideas and a decent portion of them will fail. That's OK! Failure is fine, but denial is not. Denial of failure equates denial of learning. Quick acceptance of failure is what keeps a web marketing program profitable.

In order to keep moving towards growth, constant experimentation requires objectivity when reporting results. Be willing to be wrong (if you are). Refusal to accept failure is where expensive mistakes happen, mainly because they are unnecessarily prolonged. For example, someone launches a campaign and forgets to test the landing page URL they placed in an email sent out to thousands of people. Maybe the URL is broken in the email itself, but a simple server redirect could fix it.

SEOs must fix their mistakes instead of hide them. Data can be massaged to show certain results by selectively plucking dates and random pieces of more flattering data from reports. It's an unhealthy practice to *decide for yourself* what the data should be telling you. The better approach is to form a hypothesis about what you'd like to know and then let the data tell you the answer in the most objective light.

For example, did an email drip campaign bring in more leads than the social media campaign last month? If you've deployed campaign tracking URLs, then measuring their effectiveness is as simple as comparing the two URLs in Google Analytics. If you forgot to use tracking URLs, you'll have to check the referral traffic or overall traffic (to links) used in the campaigns, and then the lead sources in Google Analytics (Figure 2-3).

*Figure 2-3. Pulling conversion by source in Google Analytics because—oops, we forgot to use a tracking URL!*

Understanding how to spot growth opportunities takes a keen eye and a taste for adventure. Recognizing quickly what's working and what's not is the most basic tenet of the growth hacker.

Aaron Ginn defines a growth hacker as:

> One who's passion and focus is pushing a metric through use of a testable and scalable methodology. A growth hacker finds a strategy within the parameters of a scalable and repeatable method for growth, driven by product and inspired by data. The essential characteristic of a growth hacker is creativity. His or her mind is the best tool in their war chest.

A very wise woman once told me that fear holds us back (and she was right). Have the guts to do what other people don't even fully understand, and get creative or as immersed in the product you're marketing as you have to. Some of the best growth hacks have involved a tie-in to product experience. Growth hackers who are empowered can see whitecaps on their growth mountains instead of just hockey sticks.

### I Got a Guy

Beware of people who proclaim "I've got a buddy who works at Google" or claim inside knowledge of any search engine by knowing a current or former employee. The whole notion that one person is key to unlocking the "secret" to SEO is flawed. There isn't one guy or gal who controls or completely understands all of the facets to an entire search algorithm.

*Don't go there.* Do not listen to these insider people or give them money or favors for stolen information. Taking random tips from people who are violating their company's NDA is not a solid strategy. Performing competitive research or composing hilarious promotional tweets for your product is more useful than chasing individuals.

Also, the people I've met who are closest to the most fun-sounding secrets (or have worked with Matt Cutts) actually *loathe* SEOs. They hate us because we are creating constant headaches for them. We're actually kind of a cool and clever crew, so it's a Road Runner versus Coyote situation. There is no logical reason an industry insider would want to make our lives easier.

Now that we've discussed the pie in the sky, it's time to get back to reality. We're pretty much all in business to make money, but the handling of it is where many organizations screw up. Care must always be given to your handling of information, money, and the power it comes with.

# CHAPTER 3

# Standards, Philosophies, and Finances

People often have commented to me about their dislike for the lack of transparency from search professionals they've worked with. Unfortunately, a proliferation of shady tools and consultants were sucked into the vacuum many years ago. It has always bothered me that SEO has a less-than-sterling image. By not employing any kind of agreed upon standards, SEO has unnecessarily experienced some *very* bad publicity. Many industry leaders took it as a changing of the tide when SEO consulting firm SEO Moz became just Moz, dropping the "SEO." The name change was likened to a symbolic tightening things up. It's like when Justin Timberlake's character in the movie *The Social Network* movie suggests going from "The Facebook" to just "Facebook." It's cleaner and represents maturation.

To ensure that SEO provides the value that it's absolutely capable of delivering, search marketers can learn from and adapt the established standards, controls, and practices of the accounting, IT, and public relations industries.

## Establishing Program Standards

Many people believe that W3C (*https://www.w3.org*), Web Standards (*http://www.webstandards.org*), and SEMPO (*http://www.sempo.org*) are the governing bodies covering SEO practices, but that's not necessarily true. Those organizations only create guidelines that are not mandatory. Standards are different than rules. Standards exist so that there's a process to ensure that what's supposed to happen is really happening. With the rise of mega-conglomerates in tech, our standards and guidelines are now being dictated *by them*. From Apple's Retina display standards to Google's project AMP (*http://bit.ly/2mfyMru*), we're being led in a weird direction. It's unclear who's setting the standards for search performance as a whole, so we now run by the engine's rules. It's cowboy times, but that's OK. We'll get there.

Best practices for an industry are simply recipes that others have successfully used before you. Standards are paramount for any website or marketing program. Standards help SEO plans stay in touch with the market over time. At the end of the day, the goal of an audit is not to punish or determine rightness, it's to provide guidance and oversight. Audits can range in size from individuals to large corporate audit departments with many full-time auditors. Independence is also important; in larger organizations, the same person shouldn't necessarily be doing the work and also reviewing the work.

In 2014, SEMPO sought to establish a code of ethics, but not much came of it. Many who participated came out opposing the code of ethics citing that it wasn't needed and could even open up SEOs to legal risks. People also felt that adhering to ethics could mean potential penalization by search engines themselves, because ethics do not *generate revenue* for the engines. This is a flawed line of logic. Measuring a piece of software might not generate any money, but *not* doing so costs even more in the end. By operating in the shadows, SEOs can risk their own reputations. The industry's reputation has suffered due to the lack of standards.

Continuing to let giant companies dictate all of the upcoming web performance standards is a dangerous road to go down. Collaboration for formation of standards vastly improves it. Philosophically the standards discussion almost always takes me back to this mid-1990s white paper:

> Linus Torvalds's style of development—release early and often, delegate everything you can, be open to the point of promiscuity—came as a surprise. No quiet, reverent cathedral-building here—rather, the Linux community seemed to resemble a great babbling bazaar of differing agendas and approaches (aptly symbolized by the Linux archive sites, who'd take submissions from anyone) out of which a coherent and stable system could seemingly emerge *only by a succession of miracles*. The fact that this bazaar style seemed to work, and work well, came as a distinct shock. As I learned my way around, I worked hard not just at individual projects, but also at trying to understand why the Linux world not only didn't fly apart in confusion but seemed to go from strength to strength at a speed barely imaginable to cathedral-builders.
>
> —Eric Steven Raymond (*http://bit.ly/2lV9cpa*), The Cathedral and the Bazaar (*http://www.catb.org/~esr/writings/cathedral-bazaar/cathedral-bazaar*)

We have to separate ourselves from the idea that change is scary and approach it in an analytical way, raising the bar for all of us. Any industry with very little or soft standards also risks becoming complicit in fraud.

I propose the following voluntary ethical best practices for organic search professionals:

- Never promise what cannot be delivered, such as guaranteed search rankings.
- Never knowingly harm a client site by violating the published search engine guidelines.

- Report data thoroughly and accurately to the best of your ability.
- Do not obtain information dubiously and pass it off as credible.
- Be transparent about any use of paid advertising or paid endorsements.
- Do not share working documents or data with third parties without permission.
- Do not employ any methods of tracking that violate the user's right to privacy.
- Never take credit for increases in search traffic that weren't verifiably related to your actions.
- Always maintain as much impartiality in reporting as possible.

I've inherited too much work over the years from colleagues who have misrepresented capabilities or simply not done anything at all. One of the worst cases was when a prospective client paid tens of thousands of dollars for what amounted to the creation of a *free Google Maps listing*. There's nothing wrong with Maps listings, but they require basic business acumen, not SEO. It takes five minutes or less to update a Google Maps listing, but that's not the most egregious issue. The *promise* made to the client by the shady consultant was to "get them to appear on page one." After a week of investigation, I could not find any other actual work performed towards SEO. The Maps listing was the consultant's cheeky way to *technically* claim credit for the client's appearance on page one.

Content and performance are the two areas of guidelines that SEO is missing. The problem with not having standards is that so many things can happen when you hire someone for SEO. Practices could be long outdated. There are industries where standards mean survival, and SEO should be one of them. Each state in the United States has a board of accountancy, which is different in every state. The American Institute of CPAs (AICPA (*http://www.aicpa.org*)) operates nationally and they have adopted the Generally Accepted Audit Standards (GAAP (*http://bit.ly/2nhTKrd*)), which governs the quality of audits. There are no SEO standards within International Organization for Standardization (ISO (*http://bit.ly/2nNullE*)) audits, which typically cover many other aspects of information technology (IT).

 You may be asking yourself what ISO stands for (but probably not). It is an international standards consortium operating in Sweden, founded in 1947 to introduce industrial and commercial standards.

The generally accepted audit concepts laid out by the AICPA are as follows:

1. The auditor must maintain independence in mental attitude in all matters related to the audit.

2. The auditor must have adequate technical training and proficiency to perform the audit themselves. The auditor must exercise professional care during the performance of the audit and the preparation of the report.

These standards give us something to think about. Quite often the consultant performing the SEO audit also stands to *benefit* if more work is needed. This is not the ideal situation for the person doing the hiring.

One of my very first consulting jobs many years ago proved a bit dramatic, because I immediately uncovered evidence of willful wrongdoing. It was clear the person hired as an SEO was not performing any type of optimizations or updates to the site. There was no change management procedure, which could have been as simple as using server logs. This person was also acting as gatekeeper to website changes and spinning all sorts of tall tales as to why changes needed to take a long time. The title of the homepage was "home"; it was not even branded with the company name. No changes showed in the server logs for weeks at a time. The company had a primitive but simple CMS that *anyone* else could've used to make their own updates. This was in a time before CMS was really a thing. What we really had was a bridge and a troll guarding it for power.

Clearly I was onto something juicy because the SEO called in sick the second day of the project and she resigned the following week, suddenly. It was probably that hair-raising project that clenched my desire to become a full-time independent SEO. It became my passion to help companies knock down what stands between them and revenue. Sometimes helping a site means drawing boundaries and making rules about how things get done: it's not always fun. Most business websites are directly tied to some aspect of generating or maintaining revenue. There needs to be processes in place so that a website can be updated as needed, so that revenue isn't lost. Another term for this is corporate governance (*http://www.investopedia.com/terms/c/corporategovernance.asp*), which is known as a system of rules, practices, and processes under which a company is governed.

Because standards vary so greatly from expert to expert, visions never quite match up. Some experts are very tied to certain tools so they will insist on switching to those for their own comfort. Switching tools to stay in your comfort zone when there's no concrete business reason to do so is poor decision-making.

What one SEO sees as a hot button issue another might see as lower priority. Ofttimes I've seen that the data from different tools doesn't line up, because data (that's relevant) often lives in the eye of the beholder. So what do we do in this situation? We call upon shared principles.

In business, GAAP is most often applied when publicly traded companies generate financial statements for the shareholders. The auditors follow the standards for reports so shareholders and investors can compare multiple companies in the same way and then make decisions. It would be amazing if one SEO could leave information intact in a way that set it up for the next one. Institutionally speaking, documentation is the strongest way to retain information. Annotations are allowed in most major platforms and can be used generously for purposes of reporting and making decisions. It's not a bad idea to have a discussion about power structure to clearly define the stakeholders for any given search program and flowchart it out.

Whether standards become established or not, most sites are not going to start out doing an *ISO 9001 SEO audit*, if such thing even exists (it doesn't). Regardless, it's advantageous to be familiar with the groundwork for compliance frameworks, in case anyone asks during an acquisition or round of investment. It's also serious self-preservation for an SEO to be able to definitively exhibit how much revenue he or she is bringing to a company.

---

### Dirty Data Gets Expensive

Attribution is never going to be 100% for all of a department's marketing activities. If subdomains or other sophisticated setups start to cause cloudiness in the funnel, spend the time to clean them up.

Data that's unattributed leads to a lack of actionable insights. Tracking URLs for campaigns are a must and they take seconds to generate.

---

Countless times I have been called upon to demonstrate for companies (or their board of directors) where revenue is coming from, precisely. Passing on revenue information is sacred and must always be handled with the care it deserves. Information you've provided about revenue may go upstream to other departments, such as accounts payable, which could then possibly trigger an audit.

It's judicious to think of revenue growth in terms of Pearson's Law (*http://bit.ly/2muFGd2*):

> That which is measured improves. That which is measured and reported improves exponentially.
>
> —Karl Pearson (*http://bit.ly/2mYE9cV*), mathematician and statistician

After speaking to and observing legions of teams operating websites, I've noticed that most organizational dysfunctions are reflected on the website itself. Let me help unpack that. I once helped a startup that had several development teams in several different countries running independent WordPress installations for the same top-level domain (TLD). One section was the corporate site; the other one was an elaborately tricked-out blog.

Both teams truly believed they were "running" the same site, even though they were doing so separately. It was like two organizations were living separate lives under the same roof. Numerous development efforts and resources were duplicated as result of separate CMS, tracking, and tool installations. The party kept on going as we uncovered duplicate tracking scripts, hosting charges, etc., which were becoming detrimental to reporting and therefore the financial health of the site. A united team is always the strongest.

I've seen so many institutional issues bring dysfunction to a website, including writing over other's website changes because people are making updates from local copies. Many smaller organizations do not have GUI monitoring tools, release schedules, or site versioning.

# Standards and Goals

Review the data. Staging servers and weekly release schedules are signs of a healthy organization following best practices. Too many procedures, however, can be onerous and actually prevent business from getting done. Part of a technical SEO's job is to determine the proper blend of running versus walking when it comes to development. It's sometimes easier to deploy a subdomain because the tools are easy to use for a blog, but then you can easily turn around and find that you're maintaining multiple tools and systems.

Just as there are no guarantees in development of what you will get when you hire a developer, the same is true for SEO. It would be ideal if a developer could just look at a site and adhere to standards for search efficacy. Wild variances in professional practice can lead to misunderstandings, disappointment, and heartache. If search professionals unite in adhering to a code of ethics, the industry could move forward and make a considerable impact. Corporations have essentially started governing standards and *that*, my friends, is one *dangerous* precedent.

Suggested standards for the SEO audit are as follows:

1. The SEO audit is performed by someone who does not benefit financially from the results, regardless of what they are.
2. The audit includes study of the search engine traffic, specifically.
3. No more than 20% of dark or direct (unattributed) traffic can be counted towards the SEO's efforts.
4. SEO effectiveness can be judged by the increase in nonbranded traffic. This means the SEO may not take credit for traffic coming from brand search unless other marketing activities are at play.
5. For ecommerce sites, data must be correlated with another source.

The first step to gaining compliance is defining what "in compliance" means. Scope has to be defined up front. There are many types of audits, which vary by size and scope. However, if you're up for sale or about to close a round of investment, you could be called upon to defend your revenue numbers and even your conclusions.

Even worse, you get audited by the IRS. The worst place to be in an audit situation is to be bereft of information. You need to know what to expect and hire a CPA if you're having any issues.

Sometimes this context is indeed the reason for getting an outside contractor. Start-ups often don't have the staff or expertise to assign more than one body to the task. If this is your use case, you probably really want to have an in-depth knowledge of this aspect of the business.

An *IT general control* demonstrates that the organization has a procedure or policy in place for technology that affects the management of fundamental organizational processes such as risk management, change management, disaster recovery, and security. *IT application controls*, which are actions that a software application does automatically, should demonstrate that software applications used for specific business processes (such as payroll) are properly maintained, are only used with proper authorization, are monitored, and are creating audit trails. IT controls are a subset of the more general term, *internal controls*.

---

## Types of Audits

There are all kinds of audits, and they range in size and scope. This is only a partial (and overlapping) list of types:

- Internal
- External
- Best practices
- Compliance
- Security
- IT
- Data integrity
- SOX
- ISO 9001

---

# Audit Trails

In accounting, an *audit trail* was originally a sequence of paperwork that validates or invalidates accounting entries. In computing, the term is also used for an electronic or paper log used to track computer activity. For example, a corporate employee might have access to a section of a network in a corporation such as billing but be unauthorized to access all other sections. If that employee attempts to access an unauthorized section by typing in passwords, this improper activity is recorded in the audit trail. In addition, the completeness of an audit determines how to reconstruct "what should have happened." In such cases, the transaction can be fixed or rolled back. Think about it in terms of a risk control. What's the risk of being wrong? It's a system, after all, so there can be no single point of failure for a search program to truly work perfectly.

Scope creep is a real thing! The pain is real, because stakeholders need to converge, not diverge, from solutions.

# Separation of Concerns

Whether publicly traded or not, there has to be a way within an organization to run marketing programs with integrity. The accounting profession has invested significantly in separation of duties because of the understood risks accumulated over hundreds of years of accounting practice. By contrast, many corporations in the United States found that an unexpectedly high proportion of their Sarbanes-Oxley internal control issues came from IT. Website marketing absolutely falls under the IT umbrella, but often it's kind of a rat's nest.

Separation of duties (SoD) is commonly used in large IT organizations so that no single person is in a position to introduce fraudulent or malicious code or data without detection. Role-based access control (RBAC) is frequently used in IT systems where SoD is required. RBAC is leveled by role exclusions, which means that roles that exclude each other cannot be assigned to the same user at the same time.

Strict control of software and data changes will require that the same person or organization performs only one of the following roles:

- Identification of a requirement or change request (e.g., a businessperson)
- Authorization and approval (e.g., an IT governance board or manager)
- Design and development (e.g., a developer)
- Review, inspection, and approval (e.g., another developer or architect)
- Implementation in production; typically a software change or system administrator

This is not an exhaustive presentation of the software development life cycle but a list of critical development functions applicable to separation of duties. To successfully implement separation of duties in information systems, the following concerns need to be addressed:

- The process used to ensure a person's authorization rights in the system is in line with his role in the organization.

- The authentication method used such as knowledge of a password, possession of an object (key, token), or a biometrical characteristic.

- Circumvention of rights in the system can occur through database administration access, user administration access, tools that provide backdoor access, or supplier-installed user accounts. Specific controls such as a review of an activity log may be required to address this specific concern.

 ### Avoid Scope Creep with Checklists

If you want to get projects done, start out with a big list and check things off. When you're done, you're done. Make a checklist and have one of more officers of the company sign off on it, and have the list reviewed and rechecked periodically.

Agree on the timeline beforehand. Is it monthly? Annually? This can be tricky since too often busy people will want to abandon the procedure, and after too long, people can forget.

Signatures mean commitment when accompanied with a report. Simply asking, "Is that what you mean? Would you mind signing here, then?" can tell you heaps about their feelings. Don't use this as a control *too often* as it could potentially freak people out.

> People need to stand up for what they are reporting. Reporting is how we maintain credibility.
>
> —Arlette Hart (*http://bit.ly/2n7Ag4A*), data scientist, FBI

It would be awesome if everyone embraced and understood *hardcore logic*, but that's not the world we live in. There are different methods to inform colleagues in an organization without confusing them. A key method to maintaining integrity is visualization, which helps organizations to begin parsing information for all parties involved. Oh yeah, I'm talking flowcharts! To enhance understanding of data, it is useful to provide a graphical overview of the key elements in the process. These charts do not show how the data flows, but instead show what the data is and what to do with it. This can aid in understanding and/or provide a common language between different stakeholders or departments.

In the real world, each case is different and your results may vary. Having said that, most cases are more similar than they are different. Each CEO wants to think his or her data set is a special thing, but ofttimes this is not the case.

You can tailor the methodologies to the real world, but pay careful attention not to just be rubber-stamping things just to get a passing grade. The numbers won't bear out in the long run.

Let's say you're conducting a site audit. One good thing to do at the beginning is to decide on some *agreed-upon procedures (http://bit.ly/2lPqfIr)* (with the client). This allows you to "delete things from your memory bank as you go" so to speak, because once you're done with one phase of the project and it's documented, it doesn't have to be revisited. This sidesteps one potential obstacle that can bog down an audit.

---

## Grace Under Pressure

Canute the Great (*https://en.wikipedia.org/wiki/Cnut_the_Great*) was a king in Denmark during the late 900s whose subjects literally thought he could part the waves of the ocean. The story goes that he demonstrated that no man, even a king, can turn the tide by him/herself. It's actually disputed historically how and whether this actually happened, but the lesson remains true nonetheless.

Like King Canute and the waves, *the ocean will eventually win*, and you will be worn down.

What do you do if someone is pressuring you to make the result unfairly match their expectations? You cannot cave in and help propagate bad expectations. Risking your reputation isn't worth it. Here are some guidelines:

- Don't tailor the data to get the numbers you want.
- Always show the date ranges.
- Always use units when presenting data.
- Damage control. Sometimes your theories won't work out.
- Be realistic with the probabilities.

---

Information ebbs and flows all the time, but the where, how, and why it passes through various parts of the system matter. Though each practitioner takes a slightly differently flavored approach, there are some things that you can do to assist in getting to the desired outcome, such as questioning your methodology, managing expectations, and asking "What does the deliverable look like?"

Reporting becomes a giant time waster if it's not mapped out and agreed upon from the outset. Rough-and-tumble reporting leads to unsatisfactory results. Fortunately there are frameworks to follow. The next section is meant to help you create the testing framework to ensure a high quality of data integrity.

---

## Lessons Learned

A lessons learned (LL) report is a great and encouraged way to neutrally document and archive what has gone right or wrong after a project, conference, or event. The LL should give a brief overview of the project, what went wrong, and what went right. It stands to reason that if something within a previous project proved successful, then future projects could benefit from this institutional knowledge. Silly mistakes like "we all forgot to make backups before that site update" during the big launch can be

---

noted. The LL seeks to prevent mistakes from happening again and again. Project managers often keep LL documents as recorded blueprints coming down the pike.

When assembling your own LL documents, the most important part to remember is that they are *never* to be used as an instrument of blame. Remember to frame obstacles in terms of problems, not people. You should equally accept input from all team members, regardless of rank. By keeping an open mind and accepting all input, the process should attempt to remain as unbiased as possible. If there's even a whiff of punishment or retribution in the document, this will defeat the purpose by freezing out the useful feedback.

# The CAVi(a)R Test

There's an easy-to-remember mnemonic that I use to ensure the highest data integrity for every site. *CAVi(a)R* is the gold standard of data integrity. It covers the entire pipeline of methods to ensure reproducibility for the enterprise. The test seeks to help prove that data is *complete, accurate, valid, and restricted* and it's fun to take out on the field.

You always want to have a plan when verifying data integrity, but sometimes the tests do not work out. Reproducible results are salient; however, it's not good to do Monday morning quarterbacking in real life. Campaigns can fail. Do not spend too much energy on the instant replay if something breaks down. You can't replay time.

## Complete

While manual data entry is sometimes necessary, most processes should be automated so the entire system will become *complete* and *defined*. "Complete" refers to the entire data flow of the applicable system or systems, not just one iteration of a process or a bunch of one-offs. When data integration is seamless between systems, reporting can become easier, more automated, and therefore reproducible. The converse is also true, where, if reporting is not reproducible, data integration will always be cast in doubt. No one can hit a moving target without the whole field in view. I *cringe* when I see SEOs filling in spreadsheets for weekly reports by hand.

So if piecemeal data doesn't cut it, why not just sign up for an all-in-one solution like Salesforce or Mixpanel and be done with it? Sadly, unless you're a larger company, the work involved in getting one of these systems up and running can often be more work than gains. Many toolsets now feature integration with other toolsets. Unfortunately, there's not usually a good way to shortcut understanding the data involved. Strategic plugins can reduce friction and custom programming. As always, diagrams are your friend here, because the clearer the better.

## Accurate

Programmers have a classic adage for this one: Garbage In, Garbage Out. If you can't trust your primary data coming in, its extremely difficult to determine when your conclusions are incorrect; you begin looking for truth inside of lies. If the information you're reporting is inaccurate, you can't wave a magic wand to fix that afterwards. Indeed, sometimes by the time it is reported, it is too late.

Proceeding with inaccurate data is a fool's gambit, to be sure. Never pretend. If you know that your conclusion may be unfounded because the data coming in or the methodology to compute the data are wrong, you have an ethical duty to your client to let them know.

Ask yourself the following:

- Is your data accurate?
- Are your methods watertight?

Both must be true. You'd be shocked to discover how often this isn't the case.

## Validity

Passing the validity part of the test means someone must manually verify at least some of the data. This includes the output data as well as inputs. Humans must periodically review at least *some* of the results! We, as SEO professionals, also have to take part in this process. Correlation is one tried and true data verification method. For example, Google Analytics is telling you there were 500 visitors to the page in one day and 40 of them converted into leads. You know that you can either check your logs for the visits or check your database for the leads—ideally both would be performed. Most developers I've worked with groan at the notion of pulling server logs and for good reason: most sites are not set up to wade through this information even if it has the data you desire. (Perhaps this will change in the future.)

## Restricted Access

Everyone in the world does not *and should not* need to have access to your data. Protect your passwords by creating and following procedures. If you are maintaining user information or any type of payment or home address information, this must be restricted, which can be super difficult in today's ultra-connected environments—but that doesn't mean you just give up. Always use protected mechanisms to store things that matter or things you're working on in predetermined secured document stores (either local computers or cloud storage). Just as you would not leave your house or car keys laying around, treat client information with precisely the same level of vigilance.

*Chain-of-custody* (COC) is the path that data (or any asset, really) follows through the organization in terms of "who owns it at any given time" (provenance). Data must come in from a known, trusted source. Each link in the chain must also be a known, trusted agent.

If this is true, then the chain of custody is preserved and the data integrity will not be compromised. If even *one* link in the chain becomes broken, then the whole thing is broken and can't be fixed. There is no *half-broken* chain. The map of who will have responsibility of the data coming through the organization is also called the *chain of responsibility* (COR).

Financial integrity of a site is crucial to its health. Understanding where the money is being spent on a site can be the difference between making a profit and total failure. Fortune may favor the bold, but luck favors the prepared.

### Money Matters

If you're bringing revenue into a company and they actively look for reasons to late-pay you or haggle after the fact, then move on from the project quickly. An easy method to measure the future health of a project is to look at the company's overall financial situation.

Is everyone working on the project being compensated in a timely way? If not, move on. The check is not in the mail. Intentions do not pay bills. People get fired, companies go under, anything can happen.

## Assessing Value for Organic Traffic

There are rare cases when scandal breaks or news is made and then traffic soars. Who takes credit? It's often difficult to assess the value of publicity. A question I've been asked many times is: how do you assess the value of just the traffic? Logically it's not hard to understand the value organic traffic brings in terms of revenue, but what about when it's mixed? When there is no ecommerce, it's not straightforward to assess the value of organic traffic. I've adapted formulas from our cousins in PR and devised a proprietary method to tabulate the value.

The first method to assign values to organic traffic is to make sure analytics is tracking commerce properly to calculate costs per lead or inquiry, etc. Design your KPIs and build your analytics reports to address those KPIs (i.e., a signup with the attached sourcing of that signup). In Google Analytics, once a financial value is attached to a KPI or lead, then you can calculate from there.

The second method to assess the value of organic traffic is brand versus nonbrand. Tracking organic queries to the site will allow for this style of analysis. If revenue transactions are happening on the site from organic traffic, the reports will match the lead sources back to it.

The third and final method to assess organic value is the public relations standard. This method is ideal when there's no ecommerce for the site or the site operator needs to assess the value of traffic for a third party. For decades, PR professionals have assigned dollar values to the exposure they gain clients by equating eyeballs on the page to advertising value (*http://bit.ly/2mR6uSO*) rates for the same placement. Online advertising rates are what a company would pay for traffic to their site; it's only logical that views can be monetized. You can make educated guesses about whether or not organic mentions are indeed more valuable than paid placement and apply multipliers. Some PR mavens take the value of advertising traffic and multiply it 2.5 times for magnification.

Sometimes you can look up a site or site tier and figure out the advertising costs; some even list it. Most publishers do not list their numbers, so it's going to require a touch of sleuthing.

We must first assess the traffic for the sites based on data from analytics itself (or Quantcast). The total ad value number is the amount of circulation to compare against the value of paid placement for the same caliber of sites. Social mentions are quantified financially in terms of search engine display ads (Google), because that is essentially how they function. Google's ad reach for certain types of ads are measured in a unit called CPM, or *cost per M* (one thousand). The suggested bid is calculated by taking into account the costs per click (CPCs) that advertisers are paying for this key-word for the location and search-network settings selected. The amount is only an estimate, and the actual CPC may vary based on competition.

To calculate traffic, simply look up Quantcast or Alexa ranking data for traffic approximations. The total ad value number is the amount of circulation to compare against the value of paid placement for the same caliber of sites. Table 3-1 illustrates how to apply the calculations to assess value of traffic.

*Table 3-1. Calculation table*

| Type of outlet | Number of mentions | Monthly uniques in the USA | Total circulation reach per day | CPM | Total ad value of medium exposure per day |
|---|---|---|---|---|---|
| News | 1 | 7,558,420 | 251,947 | $150 | **$37,792.05** |

We can take the circulation by day and divide by 1,000 to get the right variable for the CPM calculation:

251,947 / 1000 × $150 = $37,792.05

If I wanted to follow the more optimistic of the two PR standards and call this a big magnifier, I would take $37,792.05 x 2.5 for the value. There is no hard and fast rule about your magnification of paid placement versus organic, so it doesn't hurt to show both.

As an example of social value, imagine a company that had 1,000 Twitter mentions in a month and 99 of those were branded. One can calculate the total number of followers of those accounts who posted the mentions—a laborious task. As an example tally of follows let's suppose the total reach of those tweets was roughly 200,000 people. Using a conservative CPM of $5, those mentions were worth $1,000 to that organization. This is how Radian6 (*http://www.marketingcloud.com/products/social-media-marketing/radian6/*) and other industry analytics tools place value on a mention.

One can never be too removed from one's *own* calculations and interpretations of what they mean. Devise your own calculations of what success looks like and use tools to help with the heavy lifting.

Tools may come and go, but they help tell us the value of things. Like a kid in a candy store, it's time to get excited—we're about to shop for tools!

# CHAPTER 4

# Tools for SEO Measurement and Beyond

SEO helps interested visitors find a site they're looking for; site interactions help to generate revenue. Repeating the same marketing processes needlessly eats up time and fails to generate real gains. Tools have the potential to save everyone time and money. There is no tool that can perform every function of an SEO's job, but there are many that try to. It takes a village—*of tools*—to run or at least supplement a search program.

Competitor research alone can eat up monotonous hours as you compare one to another and assess the search warfare. Another task that eats up time without tools is checking for broken links. A myriad of broken links can create a negative user experience, hurt rankings, and therefore decrease revenue. There are nameless time-consuming, yet necessary, management tasks that tools can help with.

## Machine Versus Humans

The game of SEO became much more interesting for marketers when the tools began to became more sophisticated in the late 2000s. Concepts like Pagerank and Moz Trust rank began to come to the forefront. Tools gave birth to the generalist SEO whose daytime job was once pure marketing in the classic sense. Mastery knowledge of tools can play a heavy part in success.

There are simply more digital apparatuses out there on the market than can be tinkered with by *yours truly*, so I'll limit this chapter to tools I have personally used. Some folks shudder at disclosing their tools and I am one of them. The reason is not that I fear losing my job, but rather I do not wish to endorse any tools, *ever*. First of all, I do not want to make endorsements, even if I'm advising the company formally. Secondly, I am constantly experimenting and changing tools.

There have been times when I have built my own tools at the agency or tested a friend's tools. Things can quickly take a turn towards chaos at any company, especially a startup. Overnight I've seen rich companies become poor and vice versa, good tools break, and partnerships fall through (losing data). Inclusion of *any* tools in this chapter should not be seen as an endorsement, but rather as information based on experience in the field.

It's a tightrope all SEOs walk: whether or not to disclose work for other companies done with tools. If you decide *not* to disclose, you may have to maintain those third-party tools in your arsenal of tricks, which can get costly.

I have fallen in love with features and tools that, just like a *bad boyfriend*, have hurt me so, so badly. They played with my heart, but of course they totally didn't mean it, baby. Allow me to add some context. Many years ago, Raven had an amazing scrape-y keyword tool that let you run all sorts of useful keyword reports. We could look at organic SERP rankings side by side and track progress. Then something randomly changed within the walls of Google: they stepped to Raven for noncompliance with their updated agreement. Almost overnight, the sweet, sweet feature disappeared.

The choice was simple to the Raven team, which they detailed in an open letter to customers. My point in all this is that tools are always part of the SEO's journey, but nothing is forever. It's a good idea to familiarize yourself with more than one primary tool. A common theme with SEO overall, but especially in tracking and execution, is diversification. For social posting, I once fell madly for the hot new tool at the time and got burned by repeated failures to post. The result was that we crawled back to a good ol' unsexy reliable tool that meant we had to manually post images.

New analytics companies rise and fall incessantly, but none have *yet* to replace the role of human ingenuity.

---

## Feedback Matters

One of the sweetest parts about using new tools is providing feedback to the creators. In the past ten years or more, I've been a beta tester for new features of OS X Server, Google Analytics, Twitter, LinkedIn, and Facebook ads. Some of this access was granted because of who I worked with previously, but they kept giving me access in almost all of those platforms because of the feedback I provided. Usually it's via email, but I've even gone up to the team manning the booths at tradeshows and talked to them directly.

When a company is new enough, you're probably going to speak to a founder in their booth. It could be an exciting experience for them if you've used their tool extensively, as most founders relish free feedback. I also love going to demo nights for startups and meeting the founding teams to ask questions, give encouragement, or offer

---

advice. Most communities with a tech crowd have some kind of demo night, sometimes even by industry.

You'd be surprised how giving applied experiential feedback to the team creating the tools can get you behind-the-scenes access to new features and information *nobody* else has. For years, people have accused me of having some secret sauce, which is how it appears from the outside when your performance numbers are dramatically better than other people's numbers. Really all *the secret sauce* meant was being dialed in. Being a good tester means exercising a little generosity with your time (for the right platforms) and exerting effort to cultivate meaningful insights, sometimes sending screenshots and other useful documentation.

We're going to start with analytics tools, because an SEO without a firm grip on analytics is one without vision. I do not need to sell analytics because they sell themselves; however, they are never going to be the complete solution. Attention must always be paid to data integrity. Executing a plan means you must also report on it. When done right, analytics reporting is fairly smooth and automated. Hand-done reports are the enemy of an SEO and should be avoided with caution.

# Analytics

Tracking data with analytics is the most indispensable function of an SEO. An SEO has to be the master of data within his or her organization. Most organizations cannot afford a full-time data scientist or team of statisticians. Therefore, the search practitioner must own the data-reporting function if nobody else does.

Search dominance rests upon understanding the search landscape well enough to snare the visitor successfully into your funnel. It's no longer good enough to bring raw traffic to a site (in most cases); today's marketer must bring *converting* traffic. It can be very tempting to purchase cheap traffic from resellers or marketplaces like Fiverr (*http://www.fiverr.com*), but how does an organization tangibly benefit from that? All fake traffic does is hurt a site's overall health. Fake Instagram followers may make us feel good because the numbers are higher, but engagement numbers will *always* be low or nonexistent.

SEOs must test everything, and to test, you must measure. Typical testing options for campaigns, paid search, and homepage conversion experiments are A/B or multivariate (MVT). Many marketing folks have adopted the terms A/B test and multivariate test in their language, but I've found many misuse the terms. An *A/B test* is testing two or more creatives with *a single* change to the creatives, nothing more. I've heard many people say "A/B" when there are two entirely different campaigns. *Multivariate tests* are, well, *multiple variable* tests.

The goal of the MVT is to determine which combination of factors results in the conversion on the web form. The MVT formula is roughly:

> [____ of Variations on Element A] (X) [____ of Variations on Element B] (etc.) =
> [Total ____ of Variations]

So let's say we have two variations of a hero banner graphic (A) and two variations of a limited-time offer (B). In this case, you'd have *four* separate MVTs running.

Trends vary year to year for what companies are looking to understand about their web traffic. I've seen trends yo-yo back and forth between individual user-level data to general trend data on all website visitors. In 2016, the trend has become to follow the sometimes ethereal *customer journey*, merging offline and online behaviors for an individual. Unless a website has a shopping cart, individual user-level data is cool to have (while creepy), but not necessarily critical. After trying anything new, the critical part is to measure the results with as much detail as possible. The winning offer and adjoining creative will be the ones that capture the right fish.

Perfunctory data capture is useless because it's more important to know first what you need to understand as an institution. Is it the effectiveness of an offer or leads from a PPC campaign? I see many organizations try to track everything, some using multiple tools, but ultimately finding the path to shared outcomes with the data will lead to the insights that become useful. For example, you say to yourself "I think we will sell more fake mustaches if we put blogs out there featuring cute cats wearing mini mustaches." Therein lies the data collection challenge! Use tracking URLs for the cat mustache campaign, then study the conversion data accordingly. Voila! That's going to be far more effective for you to understand than to try and read analytics as though it's *The New York Times*.

## Google Analytics

Google Analytics (GA) is the most widely used analytics tool on the web, because it has captured the market share for tracking web traffic at a total of 6.1 percent (*https://w3techs.com/technologies/overview/traffic_analysis/all*) of all sites on the platform.

GA is free and very powerful when customized, and then can be coupled with Google Webmaster Tools (WMT). In terms of negatives, there are a few for GA. Organic search queries mostly disappeared from Google Analytics in 2014. The reason given by Google was an increased need to keep information secure. The organic search queries do exist within Google Webmaster Tools, but finding the data is not an intuitive process (Figure 4-1). One could argue that Google's tools in general are not user-friendly—just look at G+! Yeah, I took it there.

| 1. (not provided) |
|---|

*Figure 4-1. Good news—it's not just you! This is the ever-frustrating, omnipresent "not provided" field, which accounts for majority of organic search traffic in GA.*

 **About That Organic Search Term Data**

Google has made it a lot harder to figure out what keywords lead to conversion, but it's still possible. Several years ago, the majority of keyword data was taken out of Google Analytics. It's a common belief that this meant the end of the road for understanding keyword traffic on the organic side, but that's not true.

Google Webmaster Tools contains *all of your organic queries* and by separating them out, it's harder to form a user-specific level of data. There are custom segment reports to filter out the pesky "not provided."

Deploying an analytics suite is almost always more complicated than installing a tracking script and waiting for the magic to happen. The most common reason that companies struggle with analytics is the lack of understanding in setting it up. For example, if you have multiple links on your homepage to the same URL, it will need special handling. GA has a feature called event tracking (*http://bit.ly/1KZG4Ha*), which will allow the analytics person to measure the difference in traffic to the same URLs. That way, In Page Analytics will provide useful insights. Event tracking can also be used for pesky interactive elements, AJAX, etc.

Another example of where companies can gain more from GA is with dashboards and custom reports. There's actually a marketplace for dashboards and reports that are prebuilt and easily accessible with a few tweaks.

The most important thing to set up with regard to GA reporting for lead generation are goals (*http://bit.ly/2mxXiFr*) and campaign tracking (*http://bit.ly/2lVaTCZ*). Setting up goals in GA will allow anyone with access to run all sorts of reports on lead sources, etc. and sometimes in a way that can surprise you. Most companies are surprised to learn that top lead sources aren't always what they expected! Hey, maybe it wasn't that killer email newsletter you worked for a week on that brought in those leads but rather the smaller more targeted email campaign. Without proper tracking, these specific revelations become harder and harder to discover. Knowledge and forethought will always lead to greater insights.

## Direct Traffic in Analytics: Where Things Can Go Wrong

The mishandling of subdomain tracking scripts and comingling of content distribution networks (CDN) with SSL and non-SSL traffic is the most common reason analytics suites report having *unattributed, dirty,* or *dark traffic.* Poor mobile attribution is also a common cause for lack of data.

Incorrectly attributed traffic means that it gets munged somewhere, and most commonly shows up in GA sourced as *direct traffic* under referrals. If a website's analytics shows *direct traffic* as its top type of traffic, it generally means *something* isn't capturing correctly. People always want to think their site visitors are the exception, that they know about the company so they do just type in the URL. That's not actually how it works. Most people in the industry assume that no more than 20% of direct traffic is people actually typing URLs in. We do not know this to be fact, but it's what me and my colleagues have used as a hard and fast rule for many years. The time to get concerned is when direct or dark traffic surpasses 50% of all traffic referrals, which is highly unlikely and therefore a sign something is wrong.

Unless there's a huge ad spend (crazy money), it's unlikely for a lot of people to type in a URL directly. The delta of accepted real direct traffic percentage many of my colleagues accept and use is 20%. This means it's generally accepted by some SEOs in Silicon Valley that only 1/5 of direct traffic is going to be people typing a URL into the browser. The rest of the direct traffic is misattributed or dark traffic.

Mixing SSL and non-SSL traffic is very common with the proliferation of tools and sites that host content on their servers (i.e., CDN). Anytime you're passing secure traffic (SSL) to nonsecure, you're going to see a disproportionate amount of direct traffic. By nature of being secure, no session data will travel with a user from secure to nonsecure environments. Mixing these two together is extremely common and poses a data loss issue many organizations experience.

There are certainly dominant players in the analytics game, but there will never be just one. There are some leading website analytics tools to discuss, such as Optimizely, Mixpanel, KISS Metrics, and Unbounce. These tools will work to fill small to medium website analytics needs as well as ecommerce and mobile app tracking. My experiences with Optimizely and Mixpanel have been somewhat lackluster, however they are revered by a plethora of people.

## Optimizely

Optimizely (*https://www.optimizely.com*)'s decided strength is in its ability to do A/B testing, personalized reporting, and MVT via an easy WYSIWYG editor. The ease of use with Optimizely has led some to believe that the tool is an introductory one; when setup correctly, significant user-level data can be unmasked. I've also found the custom user segments to be quite handy, and they can actually be reused for future experiments. One downside is that it's difficult to integrate data from GA with this tool. It's no surprise that many tools do not play well together. Of all the tools in the section, Optimizely has just 0.1 percent of total internet usage.

## Mixpanel

Mixpanel (*http://www.mixpanel.com*) is very strong at tracking mobile app optimization and analytics, as well as push notification A/B testing. Many developers like Mixpanel, with the only caveat being that there are usability and documentation shortfalls. The reports and charts that come from Mixpanel are a strong point of this platform. I've seen them used everywhere from SlideShare on LinkedIn to investment decks presented to Venture Capitalists. Those who get the most out of this tool have created optimized workflows. Less than 0.1 percent of sites utilize Mixpanel as an analytics platform.

## New Relic

New Relic (*https://newrelic.com*) differs from the others in that it's providing analytics for more than just the web, offering intelligence about mobile applications. Their adoption is fairly low at 0.2 percent of the internet. By including data surrounding the mobile app experience, this platform is emerging as more popular year over year. The downside is that many smaller organizations find New Relic cost-prohibitive. New Relic does require a somewhat laborious deployment process, but this is true anytime multiple data layers are involved. Competitors to this type of tool include Sumologic, Apsalar, and AppsFlyer.

## KISSmetrics

KISSmetrics (*https://www.kissmetrics.com*) is in a league with Mixpanel, although the company has a slightly controversial past. At an early point in KISS's existence in 2011, they were a little too good at tracking data. The company was sued for allegedly re-creating cookies after people deleted them and tracking people who were using blockers.

Despite the controversy, KISS is a powerful tool for the intermediate user and their tech support has a good reputation. The KISS click-to-track feature allows for easy event and/or action tracking without complicated setup.

## Honorable Mentions

CrazyEGG (*http://www.crazyegg.com*) is another analytics tool created by the co-owner of KISSmetrics and deserves an honorable mention. CrazyEGG offers an uncommon way to interpret traffic data with heat maps. Examining what people do and where their eyes go on a site is very different than looking at the page they exited. While heat maps are not your typical analytics, the data that heat maps provide can be invaluable in understanding user site flow. Alternatives to CrazyEgg that get the job done are Hotjar (*https://www.hotjar.com*) and ClickTale (*https://www.click tale.com*). I've found the Hotjar user recordings really interesting in mapping out how people consume content.

The more you understand about the user journey, the more you're able to iron out any potential usability issues. The new term for *funnel* is *journey*, which is probably because the focus is now making sites more experiential.

### Privacy Matters!

When handling other people's information, there is a responsibility to keep it private. While it's fair game to utilize data posted on Twitter and the social graph in general, there is a line. There is no key benefit in breaking trust with your website visitors in a way that harms their privacy. Also, despite the trend of collecting data at all costs, the risks do *not* outweigh the benefits to break the law. Reselling data collected under false pretenses is *highly unethical*. People do not take kindly to their personal information being shared, which also makes it susceptible to online fraudsters looking to do all sorts of not nice things for financial gain.

Services like Leadlander (*http://www.leadlander.com*) that do reverse IP address lookups on website users to gain information are useful but not too intrusive. Make sure that any company you use operates above board; ask where their operations are based. What wouldn't be OK, for example, would be to carelessly store the user information collected on a public site without a password.

## The All-in-Ones

Everyone wants to build a lead machine. Companies want to know that when they put X amount of dollars in, they will get X times percentage returns on the investment. There are so many Swiss Army tools that profess to *do it all*. I refer to the larger suite of marketing tools as Swiss Army knives, because they seek to solve a variety of marketing problems. Tread carefully around Swiss Army knives; they do not necessarily benefit SEO, but *sometimes* they can.

There are automation tools out there that save companies time and money. Beware of *any* tools that require leisurely (expensive) consultants to sell or deploy. Does the tool require a dedicated person to utilize all of the features? That's a serious commitment for any organization to make. Especially beware of any tools requiring large upfront commitments like annual contracts. The best tools will offer a discount for annual commitments, but they seldom require it. It's important to watch for the amount of upfront commitment they require and the difficulty to maintain them. A good system should support your efforts, not the opposite, which I have seen many times.

When having discussions about analytics, it's fair to include the Swiss Army knives—Marketo, Hubspot, Eloqua, Pardot, etc. If you happen to work at a larger company and have a goodly sized sales team to support, then an all-in-one solution proves useful.

# Hubspot

Hubspot's (*http://www.hubspot.com*) defunct website grader tool was once one of my favorite diagnostics. Their free tools have always been handy. The Hubspot blog is a useful resource to folks at many levels of experience and is therefore definitely worth following. I do not think that Hubspot greatly benefits SEO as they require you to host content on their servers in lieu of your own. Paid search is one of the more compelling cases for Hubspot, because landing pages can be duplicated quickly. The landing page tool that Hubspot offers is a little confusing for me personally but once you get a hold of it, it's relatively smooth. The analytics do not integrate easily with Google Analytics or others.

# Pardot

Pardot (*http://www.pardot.com*) is a tool that allows for the quick creation of landing pages, emails, and web forms. The lead scoring and nurturing features of Pardot make it appealing to large teams or companies with complex sales processes. The feature that seems to excite people the most is lead scoring as this means the sales funnel is being automated. *Lead scoring* is the process of determining sales readiness by combining sales and marketing information. It's not as easy as it should be to duplicate landing pages and get them out quickly.

# Marketo

Marketo (*http://www.marketo.com*) is one of the most traditional and well-known marketing automation systems, and it's also fairly popular. Because there are so many rich features, the ease of use has suffered, making it difficult to quickly deploy simple things like email campaigns. People really like the audience segmentation features, and the level of automation for the sales process can provide useful insights. The weak point is customer service; many clients have complained that it's hard to get individual help. Most companies I've seen that deploy Marketo also have a consultant to work with them on it.

## Eloqua

Eloqua (*http://www.eloqua.com*) is strong on email delivery and marketing systems automation. Eloqua has caused many organizations I've worked with some pain. This behemoth tool requires a dedicated full-time person to manage it or a consultant. Marketing resource management (MRM) is a feature that few systems have, but it's very useful to be able to easily update assets (forms, scripts, etc.). When comparing true MRM systems to Eloqua, the tool falls short, but to have that functionality at all is a benefit to most organizations.

## Honorable Mention

Customer.io (*https://customer.io*) also gets an honorable mention here. The tool has free plans and reasonable pricing for its paid plans. While you're paying less to get started, it does take more muscle to set up this one. If you're looking for a lot of customization with your automation, this tool will deliver if you have the right developer resources.

### Test Tools Yourself

Always test tools yourself before testing them on someone else's site. Unless you have an overwhelming amount of assurance that a tool is legitimate, do not recommend it to someone else.

When I use a new social monitoring tool or service, I test it on a personal handle. If I test a tool to manage my Twitter following, for example, I can get a good sense of how it will impact the magnification and appearance of the account across many different mediums.

# Research Tools

The very *coolest* place to start any SEO program is with competitive landscape research. The challenges are unique! It's nothing but advantageous to understand the battlefield your competitors are interested in conquering. If a competitor is further along (i.e., more prolific in terms of search saturation), you will only stand to benefit from investigation. There's an infinite amount of research information to consider for search, so this is where tools truly get to shine. Be careful of tools that try to tell you what conclusions to draw from research itself; they lead to siloed thinking.

When performing SEO research, the first place to look is in the web browser itself, whether it's your site or someone else's. Go ahead and view the site source—it's OK. You don't have to be a developer to glean useful information.

Look at the website's title, meta description, and any listed keywords (Figure 4-2). They tell you the positioning and goals for the site. There's no appreciable SEO value to meta keywords any longer, but they're good for tipping off the competition.

```
<title>O'Reilly Media - Technology Books, Tech Conferences, IT Courses, News</title>

<!-- Google Plus Link --><link href="https://plus.google.com/108442503368488643007" rel="publisher" />

<meta http-equiv="Content-Type" content="text/html; charset=UTF-8">

<meta name="varify-v1" content="abK30/05baixwH0IC3Oolk1/zLsPjzlrlhtTr2EYLuU=" />
<meta name="keywords" content="O'Reilly, oreilly, technology books, technology conferences, IT training courses, tech news" />
<meta name="description" content="O'Reilly spreads the knowledge of innovators through technology books, online services, and tech conferences. Find the
technology resources you need at O'Reilly Media, a technology company at the leading edge." />
<meta name="twitter:card" content="summary" />
<meta name="twitter:title" content="O'Reilly Media - Technology Books, Tech Conferences, IT Courses, News" />
<meta name="twitter:url" content="http://www.oreilly.com" />
<meta name="twitter:description" content="O'Reilly spreads the knowledge of innovators through technology books, online services, and tech conferences. Find
the resources you need at O'Reilly Media, a technology company at the leading edge." />
<meta name="twitter:image" content="//cdn.oreillystatic.com/oreilly/images/oreilly-social-icon-120.png" />
<meta name="twitter:site" content="@OReillyMedia" />
<meta property="og:title" content="O'Reilly Media - Technology Books, Tech Conferences, IT Courses, News" />
<meta property="og:type" content="website" />
<meta property="og:url" content="http://www.oreilly.com" />
<meta property="og:image" content="//cdn.oreillystatic.com/oreilly/images/oreilly-social-icon-200.png" />
<meta name="language_name" content="English"/>
<meta name="native_language_name" content="English"/>

<link href="http://www.oreilly.com" rel="canonical" />
<link rel="shortcut icon" href="//www.oreilly.com/favicon.ico" />
```

*Figure 4-2. Note that the O'Reilly website uses a meta title, keywords, and description on their public website.*

It's generally useful to review further to find out what analytics tools the competition is using. This will give you a sense for how much of an investment they're making into their search presence.

To embark upon research beyond the browser is a wise idea. Brand competitor research tools I've used are SEMRush (*https://www.semrush.com*), Ahrefs (*https://ahrefs.com*), and Moz (*https://moz.com*). No one in particular stands out above the other, because it depends on your use case. It can be difficult to find the right tool for the job sometimes, but that's a compelling reason for testing multiple tools and taking advantage of any free trials.

## Serpstat

For a different type of research dive, consider checking out the deep cuts from Serpstat (*https://serpstat.com*), which encompasses all sorts of fun information. Their free trial gives simple at-a-glance information on search rankings for certain keywords alongside the paid competition and interest.

## Scrapebox

Scrapebox (*http://www.scrapebox.com*) is a bit of an ugly duckling in terms of usability, but that almost endears it to SEOs who like it anyway. The amount of growth-hack-ish functions Scrapebox provides to the user is really interesting, from checking domain availability to creating sitemaps or scrape emails. This tool goes so far as to use proxies to hide from mother Google what's happening in your research. In particular, the meta information and keyword scrapers are useful to automate competitive research among other things. Critics of Scrapebox have gone so far as to call it black hat, but that depends on how it's used.

# SEO Diagnostic Tools

The following tools are used to diagnose the health of a website's SEO program. Diagnostics aren't always as straightforward as they seem. Just like with research tools, it's advantageous to try a few at once to see what *feels right*. Also, be sure to run diagnostics on more than just the homepage! Many organizations tend to spend the majority of the time worrying about the homepage and not thinking through the rest of the site, which is a mistake. The front page starts the journey, but it should not be the destination.

## SEOptimer

SEOptimer (*http://www.seoptimer.com*) is a broad-brush initial SEO diagnostic overview tool that's free and super easy to use. Generally speaking, the SEOptimer tool shows numerous coverage areas for what's happening on a site. In two seconds, you can diagnose basic SEO health issue areas with no popups or annoying sign-ins.

## Majestic

Majestic (*https://majestic.com*) offers a quick diagnostic that takes seconds to use, which includes a largesse of information on links and domains. The Majestic tool will tell you for free how many backlinks you have, including a breakdown of the history in addition to topics, ref domains, and anchor text. In order to drill down on specifics in key areas, you will need a monthly Majestic subscription.

## Chrome Developer Tools

Chrome Developer Tools (*https://developer.chrome.com/home/devtools-pillar*) audits are my most treasured diagnostic SEO tool, because it provides very specific detail on website performance. With an increased importance on execution, it's really handy to run a developer-focused audit. The tool allows you to drill down on the specifics, which are linked to the assets in question.

Figure 4-3 shows some recommendations to improve website performance and utilization of the network. Keep in mind that the unused CSS rules could actually be used by other pages than the one you're on; this test is only for one page (the one you're viewing as you run it). When running diagnostics, they will generally tell you if you're examining just one page or multiple pages. If you're deciding whether or not to act on the performance issues, consult someone with website development knowledge if you're unsure. Some performance errors matter far more than others.

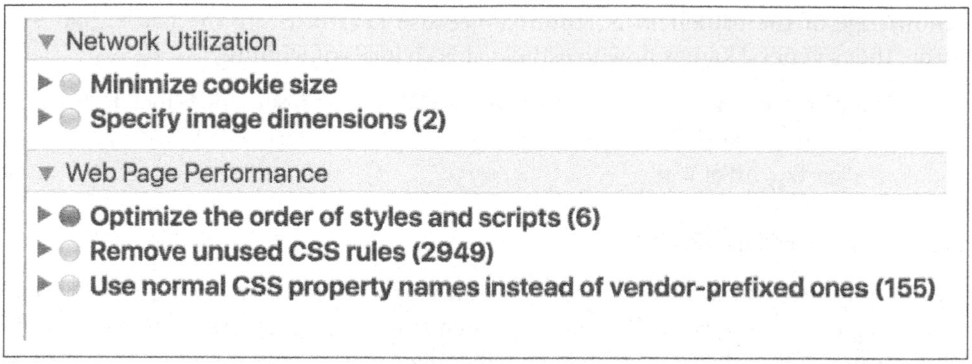

*Figure 4-3. This is an example set of suggestions from a Chrome Developer Tools audit.*

# Keyword Research Tools

One of the most meaningful keys to understanding search behavior is keyword research combined with the accumulation of topical knowledge. Sometimes keyword targets are driven by emotional reasons like "I should own this" or "We are better than them." Other times, keyword targets start as a random guess or hunch. Balance what the site's stakeholders *think* is being searched for with research entailing what people *actually are* searching. This is where research tools come in like a shining knight of valor.

Set a goal for the keywords or a group of keywords you want to begin to rank for. There is a certain amount of fluidity to each keyword set, but overall the main goals shouldn't change too dramatically. You will pull out your hair (or someone else's) if the keyword goals change month to month. Nobody can hit a moving search target.

Let's think about creating a solid keyword goal for our beloved eagle. When shooting for page one in a search for "endangered eagle news," the addition of "endangered" is a qualifier. The qualifier is meant to help with the fact that there's palpable search engine confusion for said query. After all, the *Eagles* are a super famous music group (since the 1970s) whose members frequently make the news in addition to the Philadelphia *Eagles* football team, etc. To appear in the results for "eagle news" sounds cool on paper as a keyword goal, but it's not necessarily useful for our purposes.

It's noble to have big keyword dreams; however, the project's size and resources should scale to your level of boldness and appetite for risk. If my daytime job were purely to market my *eagle conservation* site and I had a team of writers and designers, I would go for "eagle news."

Another perspective to take on is letting the industry tell you what the goals are. Use a combination of keyword tools to identify who is paying for which terms, how they're ranking, and whether or not there is space for you.

Knowledge of the battlefield is required, because keywords *are* the battle. Sun Tzu wrote that a general knows how to estimate his chances of winning.

> The general who wins the battle makes many calculations in his temple before the battle is fought. The general who loses makes but few calculations beforehand.
>
> —Sun Tzu, Art of War

## Google Keyword Planner

The Google Keyword Planner, better known as the keyword tool (KT) (*https://adwords.google.com/KeywordPlanner*), is intended to generate ideas for paid search while showing you the costs associated with advertising. Paid search is still a facet of search, so the research can absolutely be useful. The other information to be gained from the KT is keyword *competition*. Some terms may be so difficult to rank organically that paid competition is rough; knowledge about competition matters more than the search method itself.

## SpyFu

SpyFu (*http://www.spyfu.com*) is another tool I've used for keyword and competitor research. The user experience and reports have not always been pretty, but this tool gets the job done. When tracking competitors alongside yourself, it provides another dimension of information to consider. Let's say you've optimized for local search and your competitors have not. When diverging from the pack, rankings will start to differ from the competition, allowing you to study how they comparatively improve (or don't). They provide branded reports for agencies and individuals alike; this can be tremendously useful for tracking a project's results in a way other tools do not.

SpyFu will also give you competitor alerts and good detail about their paid search. It's a good idea to set this tool up if you happen to catch someone else advertising on your turf. It's always helpful to understand where your competitors are spending money.

## SEMRUSH

SEMrush (*http://www.semrush.com*) is a well-known analysis tool with easy international research integration for about 25 countries. International SEO is very complicated and many tools created in the US focus on accessing data for the US. Just like SpyFu, SEMrush allows the user to research competitors for paid search.

## Moz

Moz's Open Site Explorer (*https://moz.com/researchtools/ose*) is also useful as a diagnostic for competitive research as well as backlink checking. Payment is not required to use the explorer. Overall, Moz is not going to give any deep insights, but it's a friendlier interface than Google's tools.

# Social Tools

Social traffic will bring tangible heat to a site when done right. Because social is such a great source of natural backlinks for the search engines, we have to care about it for SEO. Many companies will spend 5 to 10 hours creating a blog post and only 5 minutes promoting it. One of the fastest and best ways to get traffic to a site is by broadcasting it on social.

Quality of inbound site traffic waxes and wanes depending on the platform it's coming from. Twitter traffic can spend less time on site than LinkedIn, for example, because those users are most likely to be coming from mobile. While I'm a purist who likes to use the platforms themselves for social, this isn't always possible when multiple accounts and services are at play. Tools are the key to harnessing social's greatness for SEO programs.

Social monitoring tools are prevalent in the tools and analytics industries. Many companies want to understand more than how many tweets they were mentioned in. Companies want to know whether or not they're liked and how people feel about them. Tools like Social Mention (*http://www.socialmention.com*) will calculate the sentiment. There are a ton of tools that claim to measure sentiment. Sentiment analysis is far from an exact science, because most tools do not account for the greatest human communication elements like *sarcasm*. Machine learning will only improve in the coming months and years, so someday I may be eating these words.

Whether or not you happen to believe if social matters to search, we know social drives traffic. The following tools are useful for scheduling, managing, and measuring social.

## Hootsuite

Hootsuite (*https://hootsuite.com*) is the most established standalone social posting platform out there with over 10 million users. You can add a fair amount of accounts on social across a variety of platforms with relative ease. The biggest strength of the platform is its stability and ease of collaboration across teams. I've worked with many remote teams who successfully use Hootsuite to coordinate posting and monitor social accounts.

## Buffer

Buffer (*https://buffer.com*) is another very popular social posting tool that has a slick user interface and is overall fun to use. When I first started using it, they had some fun suggested tweets and a cool way to schedule posts. Unfortunately, I do not use

Buffer at work, because it's been far too unreliable in sending posts. To be fair, it's difficult to know for sure where those failures came from, whether it was them or the social platform it failed on.

Reporting on social is often difficult for organizations to get right. Simply counting the number of followers and the amount of engagement is a good way to start. I also like to look at the amount of traffic a website is getting from social.

### Don't Forget What's Authorized!

Using social tools almost always requires a login authentication with the account itself. If you're using Facebook or Twitter, for example, the social tool you're setting up will ask you to authenticate your ownership of the account.

90% of the time people stop using a social service and they forget to deauthorize the app within social. This means you are continuing to give your data to an organization you no longer get the benefit of. Anytime there is a discontinuation of a service you've authorized, go to the apps and deauthorize it (Figure 4-4).

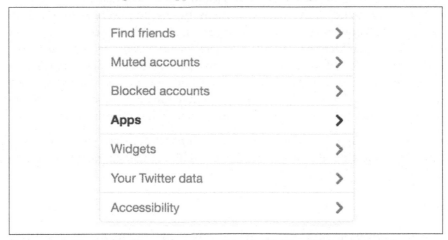

*Figure 4-4. Under Profile → Settings → Apps in Twitter. Simply hit revoke.*

## Sprout Social

Sprout Social (*http://sproutsocial.com*) is an easy-to-use social reporting tool that allows reporting for multiple social platforms. It takes seconds to run a report with nice charts that can indicate whether or not an account is doing well by showing the number of followers versus unfollowers in addition to demographics like male versus female by platform. The tool is easy to use, but there's currently no way to autoschedule reports. If you're running the same reports every week, this can be frustrating.

## Simply Measured

Simply Measured (*http://simplymeasured.com*) provides social reporting, measurement, and attribution through an easy-to-use interface. This tool also features an API that allows for integration into other areas of the business, which is really helpful when examining how social relates to the funnel.

## Cyfe

For social reporting, it's always a challenge because each program has different KPIs. There's no all-in-one social tool right now that I'm super excited about. There are some useful tools for aggregating social reports, aside from Moz. Cyfe (*http://www.cyfe.com*) is an all-in-one reporting tool that will allow you to pull everything into one easy dashboard. Many executives like Cyfe because the dashboards combine numerous platforms and are easy to understand with a slick interface. Google Analytics also does a fairly good job of all-in-one reporting if you build dynamic dashboards to track KPIs.

## Quintly

Quintly (*https://www.quintly.com*) is another dashboard-friendly tool that allows for easy reporting. The strength of this platform is in competitive monitoring and benchmarking.

There will continue to be new tools in the social space, probably more rapidly than any other area of marketing. The usefulness of a social tool is in the eye of the reporter, but make sure to never expect a tool to determine its usefulness for you. It's always the stronger position to begin with your own metrics for success (i.e., benchmarks, KPIs, and goals). With your own goals clear in your mind, the selection of the tools becomes far easier.

---

### Fun Wildcard Social Tools

Ever wonder if someone's following on Twitter is real or not? There's an app for that! Followerwonk (*https://moz.com/followerwonk*) is a Moz tool designed to assess the quality of a social following. Prepare yourself for some heartache; there are almost definitely bots all over your followings on Twitter.

Want to find influencers on social and communicate with them in a scalable way? Pitchbox (*http://pitchbox.com*) is a platform that allows for easy identification and contacting of influencers. Sites like Famebit (*https://famebit.com*) can also help you engage influencers at a scalable level.

---

# Automation

For a program to succeed on a massive scale, it must be, well, scalable. Repeating processes leads to fatigue and therefore failure. Alerts are the superlative way to automate processes, hands down. Slowly build your robot army and mold it to perfection.

## Google Alerts

Google Alerts (*https://www.google.com/alerts*) are free and take very little time to setup. They can be tricky to get right if the query you're using has multiple meanings. There are a number of services that charge for alerts, but rarely is a paid solution warranted.

## IFTTT

IFTTT (*https://ifttt.com*) is one of the most omnipotent automation tools around. With little effort, you can actually program IFTTT to do anything from turn the lights on in your house to build a Twitter user list for those who mention your handle.

Social automation for content promotion is a good idea when content is coming down the pike quickly. It's very easy to set up auto feeds via RSS with Twitterfeed (*http://www.twitterfeed.com*) or also with IFTTT. Twitterfeed is not a particularly exciting tool, but you can find an RSS for most news sites and plug them into the tool. The feed will auto share to the social channels you authorize. A good example use case is sending out the posts from a company blog. If your site has RSS set up and social posting is properly configured, this tool allows for simple auto posting.

 **Auto Posters Beware!**

It's worth the time to manually post if you're using images or attempting to support a live event. Automated tweets sent out during a live event are not a good idea unless you're keeping an eye on it. There have been many high-profile incidents of auto posts making a company look bad.

---

### Amusing Digression

Many SEOs like link-building tools, beyond Google Webmaster Tools and Open Site Explorer Tools. I do not advocate use any *auto* linking tools. Gaining links for the sake of it should not be the primary focus of any search program. The game of link building à la spray and pray doesn't work as it once did.

---

> Before embarking on any link building program, determine which authorities should care about it. Unless a competitor is sinking you, outbound linking is not necessarily a smart place to spend a majority of your time.

# Content Management Systems

The most powerful tools for managing websites are content management systems, as they allow access to all members of an organization. It's important to make sure it's easy to update content on a site, whether you're a developer or not. Sometimes companies cut corners by only placing the blog in a CMS, and not the whole site. Getting backed up on content updates is a silly problem to have. Unless you need barriers to updating content, a CMS system keeps an organization from having costly site maintenance update expenses.

There's always the temptation to go with a cookie-cutter website from services like SquareSpace, Wix, or GoDaddy. Managed services will get you going fast, but you're painting yourself into a corner. You're not really owning your environment if you're leaning so hard on someone else's. Taking a shortcut when getting started often means more work later; it's the *stitch in time saves nine* principle. A balance can be found with finding a quick solution while still owning your own content.

## WordPress

WordPress (*https://wordpress.com*) is one of the most adopted CMS platforms right now. The ease of use for WordPress is second to none; when configured correctly almost anyone can use it. There are countless SEO plugins as well. Many news organizations and very large sites are using the WordPress platform due to its stability and the amount of tools available. Platforms that have grown as meteorically as WordPress can become targets; they must be maintained and kept up-to-date for security purposes. It's also common for sites built with WordPress templated themes to have many unneeded extra files and resources.

## Prismic

Prismic (*https://prismic.io*) is a more developer-centric CMS than its competitors. Updates are automatic and you can use whatever template language you'd like. The marketplace is more open to what a developer might want to do, which makes this platform a rising star.

## Ghost

Ghost (*https://ghost.org*) is a hip new CMS, mostly known as a blogging platform. It's very popular for mobile enthusiasts, but some folks think it's unnecessarily difficult to install. Personally I like the split-screen interface; it's a fun and futuristic way to edit. If you're thinking of doing just a blog with it, Ghost is great, but you may not want to run a whole site on it.

## Joomla

Joomla (*https://www.joomla.org*) was once a developer favorite with a good community around it, but it's popularity has waned over the past few years. It's a slightly more complicated CMS than most, but still very flexible for a bigger team's usage. A major strength of this platform is its handling of multimedia and large sites. If the primary use of your site is blogging, Joomla is not your best choice.

## Drupal

Drupal (*https://www.drupal.org*) is often a favorite with developers. It was released in 2001, which makes it a teenager yet oldster of the CMS group. Theme choices are fewer than its competitors and the ease of use is nowhere near as good as other platforms.

## Medium

Medium (*https://medium.com*) is a very popular blogging platform that more and more people are excited about. Hosting your blog on Medium puts it in front of many other eyeballs; there's a captive audience. The downside is that you do not get to host your own content or have your own reporting. Without visibility, it's harder to do reporting on a potential hole in analytics.

### Templating Languages

Move aside, CSS! There's a new kid in town we all have to talk about now called *CMS templating languages*. Examples are Mustache (*http://mustache.github.io*), Twig (*http://twig.sensiolabs.org*), and Pug (*https://pugjs.org/api/getting-started.html*). This is next-level wizard stuff and worth the effort to configure.

---

## Useful WordPress Tools

Given that there's generally limited resources for web development, some SEO can be performed with handy plugins. One should shop for templates with a careful eye. Do research upfront about a WordPress theme, like how often it's updated or if the author has good reviews. One easy tip-off that you're using a theme is if you haven't changed the stock photos. The main reason to do this is to make your site your own, but also to use better image titles and compressed images.

---

In terms of all-in-one SEO tools, Yoast (*https://wordpress.org/plugins/wordpress-seo*) and SEO Ultimate (*https://wordpress.org/plugins/seo-ultimate*) are the two plugins I have seen used the most. If it's the difference between no SEO and some SEO, these plug-ins are a solid choice. Many people like Yoast, but users and bots alike tend to have issues with their sitemaps. I have had mixed experiences with Yoast, but it's great for beginners or large teams who need assistance filling in meta information with target keywords in mind. Yoast can also be used for SEO with sitemaps disabled. I find Google XML Sitemaps (*https://wordpress.org/plugins/google-sitemap-generator*) is a reliable tool for sitemap creation and management.

WP Smush (*https://wordpress.org/plugins/wp-smushit*) is a sweet way to reduce the size of images for faster load times. It's almost fun to watch the file sizes compress. Autoptimize (*https://wordpress.org/plugins/autoptimize*) optimizes source by concatenating scripts and styles, which minifies and compresses them. The plugin also adds expirations to headers, which properly caches them, moves styles to the page head, and can move scripts to the footer. When scripts are moved to the footer, they load last, reducing the time before the user can start perusing the page. It's not 100% always advisable to move tracking to the footer, like when your pages are coupled with PPC and the user clicks off too fast to load.

Accelerated mobile-landing pages are a cinch with Wordpress for AMP (*https://word press.org/plugins/amp*), and it is reasonably cool and easy to use. If you implement Google's project AMP via WordPress, it gives you a handy preview to test out prior to going live.

Honorable mention goes to Aksimet (*https://wordpress.org/plugins/akismet*), because it helps block spam and enjoys strong WP user adoption and positive reviews.

Tools are the search marketer's BFF, but things can take a turn when you don't watch the numbers consistently. There's no tool that has yet to replace human ingenuity and creativity, so a combination of tools and strategies works best. Now that you're a tools aficionado, let's get into the good stuff—building a search program that will dominate over time, despite changes in trends that arise.

# CHAPTER 5

# Setting Up Programs and Reporting

Taking the time to correctly set up an SEO program is worth the effort every time. If you're walking into an established organization, it's tempting to go along with what's already been set up. But resist temptation, because your job isn't to do what's easy—it's to increase the growth of a site.

Fuzzy data morphs into *untrusted* data, also known as *dirty data*. If you're starting a project where everyone believes the frameworks that have been set up for the site seem *trusty*, it's OK to use it—but stay vigilant because once you start to manage something, you will eventually become responsible for it. If there's an issue with something like data capture, you'll soon inherit said issue. Do your own independent investigation when it comes to data capture and analytics instrumentation. A watchful eye catches mistakes; a complacent one doesn't. I cannot stress enough that it's fair to walk in the door with some skepticism if you're being asked to take over an existing search program. *Trust, but verify.*

Whether it's a new or continuing project, you always start by determining the target, which is usually a company's website or sometimes a mobile app install or an Amazon or Etsy page. Clearly set benchmarks and physically examine the site source or landscape of the asset you're ranking for and skip this at your peril! Avoiding the code check means you are likely to miss out on key observations that will boost the program. There have been numerous cases in which I've unveiled ancient tools of the past in the source. Nobody benefits from making calls to other servers for no tangible reason. Set yourself up for success by *not* keeping too much junk in the trunk.

## Building a Growth Program to Last

A program that starts with welcoming an acceptable percentage of failure is more likely to flourish. *Without learning there is no growth, and to learn you must test.* You must produce results. The elements of a strong program include using measurement for optimization and building a site that fosters trust and transparency. Learning should be the key component in every program and includes a willingness to examine data impartially, constant research, and experimentation.

Failure happens for many reasons, but it will continue to happen in any situation where there is a general unwillingness to ask questions and recognize mistakes.

> When a great team loses through complacency, it will constantly search for new and more intricate explanations to explain away defeat.
>
> —Pat Riley (*http://bit.ly/2muLiUP*), former NBA coach

Focus should instead be on building up the institutional mindset and constant tweaking of strategies and campaigns. An example of tweaking would be when you happen to notice that last month's blogs didn't pick up much traffic, and suggest that maybe the team should spend more energy promoting them. The same amount of energy or more should be spent *promoting* a piece of content as building it. Promoting blogs could mean turning parts of them into syndicated content or writing new descriptions to post again on social channels.

Installing an SEO plugin in WordPress is not SEO. The most successful SEOs are the ones who stay focused and let the data show them the real story of what's going on. They study trends and try to steer the boat correctly, taking bets on multiple territories. Doing what's easy or out of the box will never get you to the top search spot.

Logically speaking, if you walk into a new project with almost complete agnosticism, then you are in the most likely state to be open to new ideas. If you're running a WordPress site without mobile optimizations and have tons of unneeded CSS, then it is not typically a winning enterprise.

### Phone a Friend

Some industries are unbelievably difficult and specific, so never be afraid to phone a friend with experience in any given area. Learning should always be encouraged for SEO success. One of the coolest parts I've enjoyed about being an SEO is the opportunity for cross-collaboration among many different industries. Also, it's OK to ask for SEO help, too. Most senior-level SEOs who have done it for a long time actually enjoy talking shop, whether it's about the industry, war stories, or the latest trends.

The day should always include the element of research and discovery. Decisive action cannot be taken without sufficient information. SEOs have to read every day to find good consumable information and stay up on trends. The biggest sites that thrive from organic traffic typically produce a lot of content or aggregate others' content successfully.

The two most important factors for conversion are *trust and transparency*. Without both factors present, the chances of a user engaging with a site are minimal. A good example of how to lose trust is to have mismatching page descriptions. The meta description is not a huge SEO factor any longer, but it's still the method by which your future site visitors see what's supposed to be a summary of the page. If the summary doesn't describe what the page actually contains or if it feels too generic, you will not be likely to get the click.

## Using Keyword Identification Tools

There's some wildly popular and long-running folklore about this type of research. When marketers struggle heavily on specific individual keywords, they usually lose sight of the big picture. You have to increase *overall* organic visibility before you start to focus on individual terms. While it would be nice to automate keyword research, a human element is still required. Machines do not always know the subtle differences between terms. Predictive analytics tools aren't (yet) what they should be, although there are some very cool ones out there. No one tool currently performs all of the jobs of an SEO practitioner when it comes to keyword research. I have yet to find a one-size-fits-all tool, but—alas—I prefer to use a few different tools as checks and balances.

The problem with using multiple tools is that the data will never match all the way 100%. Servers have syncing issues and varying time zones. Some tools seem to constantly change the way they display information, so it can be hard to correlate. There's a trend towards oversimplified reporting for popular platforms like Twitter, Facebook, and LinkedIn. Any tool that doesn't allow the user to download and/or export all crude information into a CSV is holding something back (your data). Otherwise, you'll have to correlate by hand, which leads to too much time spent on reporting. Automation to some degree is necessary, and we will cover that in the next section.

# Go Through the Weeds Toward Goals

There are at least a dozen marketing and development practice areas combined that legitimately fall under SEO's big hug. When you're touching the website, it's easy to get bogged down on things that are seemingly important for the company but not essential SEO. I've seen programs fail when they lose focus because they turn into grouped general marketing practices. There's no silver bullet in SEO; it's more like you're *weaving a digital quilt.* When you combine a variety of little things, the needle feels like it's moving forward when it's really not. Silly little crawler bots can be deceiving when you're looking at traffic. Even the best of us have seen false positives for indicators of growth. The trick is to find them. Course-correct quickly.

SEO goals are a thorny thing, unfortunately. Everyone should have tangible goals for a search program, but it's impossible to promote specific numbers. I've seen marketers and search folk who sometimes overcompensate when outlining their goals (in sales mode), but that should *not* include promising a hard number for growth or top place in search. Since SEOs do not have direct control over the search engines, it doesn't make logical sense to claim direct control over results.

This is where it's good to reframe the concept of what the SEO can do. A key question to always consider: what is our target goal for *overall traffic* and then also for *organic traffic*? Set a realistic goal based on the amount of assets you have (i.e., content and/or activities that are happening). If your incoming website traffic is hovering around 100 visits per day *from all sources*, is a sudden quadruple jump in organic a realistic goal? While everyone wants to achieve scalable marketing growth, it may not happen in the first few months.

When people ask me to pick a goal, I typically say we will increase conversions (sales) and the overall amount of organic search. Never promise exact percentages of growth; credible SEOs do not tend to do this. After reviewing site analytics and look-ing at the site, I can make my *own* assessment on the potential for increases. There are too many unknown factors to make assumptions about what's known. I generally don't vocalize my predictions too loudly for fear of misrepresenting results, but I can study any available analytics history and look for the factors that indicate whether growth has ever happened in the past. *Nobody* can promise definitive organic growth; they can only aspire to it. *Nobody* can explicitly guarantee traffic is coming for certain unless they're buying it.

> All growth depends upon activity. There is no development physically or intellectually without effort, and effort means work.
>
> —Calvin Coolidge (*http://bit.ly/2lxrMrn*), US president

The key to growth is watching the dials, and a clear way to do that is through report-ing. Goals should be clearly defined enough to feel "locked in" to all relevant parties; you cannot fight on a floating battleground (unless you're the Navy). An issue many SEO programs face is with reporting. My first major SEO project failed not in the SERPs but in management because I didn't pick one firm set of metrics to report on regularly for the executive team. Therefore, they had no confidence that what I was doing was working.

Over the years, I have developed my own dashboards and custom reports to demon-strate growth on a consistent basis. I tweak them and build new ones constantly while keeping physical backups in PDF form. Numerous organizations I've worked with find reporting to be one of the most difficult pieces of the program. Reporting is especially expensive to an SEO program when it isn't automated, because nobody typ-ically wants to pay for reporting time. A majority of the SEO's energy should be spent generating traffic, not bending over backward to show what they are doing.

### Haters Gonna Isolate

There are a subset of people, *sometimes* developers, who do not "believe" in the practice of SEO and therefore will want to dissect all SEO-related practices. Skeptics are present in every organization and that's OK. The antidote to this is reporting. My suggestion is to find a balance in what's being reported so all parties feel that transparency exists.

Annotate SEO-impactful changes in analytics diligently—things like updates being made to the website or the launch of a new campaign. A majority of analytics suites have a mechanism to create annotations. Reporting is most difficult when the data is incomplete; running in circles to compile information from multiple sources is an awful position to be in.

If you're pulling analytics information for a report you're presenting to others, *always* pull down a local copy or take a screenshot of what you are viewing. It's an easy mistake to pull something and forget the timeframe or maybe you're in the wrong view. Keeping a record of where it's coming from helps you maintain data integrity in reporting along the way.

# Setting Up an Organic Search Program

Whether you're SEOing a new site or an old one, this section will cover how to set up an organic search marketing program. Your goals for search have now been defined. It is now time to cross over into targeting *how* people are going to be hitting your site. It used to be good enough to harvest the potential searcher's interest, but now there's an industry-wide expectation for a search practitioner to also generate interest. The vehicle for understanding the interest of a potential visitor is the keyword.

Always consider the end point, whether the user will be buying an antique eagle figurine or downloading a white paper. You can start with research by dissection.

Keywords are not necessarily the heart and soul of search anymore (h/t algorithms), but they're still the best path to attaining search goals. Nontechnical marketers may not grok the nuances of rich snippets or server optimizations, but they'll certainly get keyword targets. When starting SEO programs, it's imperative to choose keyword targets and be clear about the audience you are trying to reach. Take the time to understand if your keyword targets are reflective of how people are *actually* searching. Look at everything from a few potential perspectives—the buyer, the researcher, the looky-loo. There should be a few personas (types) of people who could potentially visit the site you're optimizing. Mentally put yourself in their shoes. If the site you're working on existed previously, you can start with the content that is there. Look at whatever analytics might exist to assess what's performing well, if anything.

If the site is a new one, then start doing random searches for what *you would* use and find the site *yourself*. If the product or service is new and therefore undiscovered, pick what's most closely related. In a new program, you should be the most open to possibilities that don't feel as natural to you. In the beginning phases, you want to trap organic search queries, period. The true shaping of keyword goals will always come later; it's not a good idea to get caught up on "the perfect query" as that's not really *a thing*. How people find a site (or if they do at all) is always going to evolve and change. In more than 20 years of working on the web, I've never heard anyone declare, "my website is done." Done-ness on the web is also not *a thing*, especially in the search world. Ranking-focused programs often miss out on new opportunities.

The Google select window (Figure 5-1) or snippet preview window in the browser is the fastest way to see how queries are shaping up in terms of the searcher's interest. Understanding a site visitor's intention is the most powerful information to have in keyword research.

Let's take the example of our friend the eagle. In this exercise, we're looking to potentially start a new website with the goal of bringing awareness to the endangered eagle, the most majestic bird in the United States. I start typing "eagle" and the *snippet preview* starts to form:

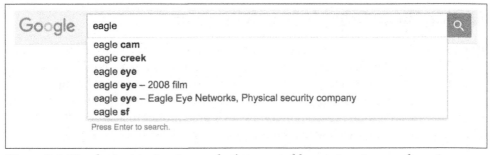

*Figure 5-1. Simply start typing to see what's suggested by most major search engines.*

OK, now we know that the eagle cam is popular in the United States. Visit different country sites (like Google.ca or Google.co.uk) if you're looking for international perspectives. After some research about the eagle cam, we see that many sites are government-run parks. Whether something is *.gov* or *.edu* matters more to Yahoo! and Bing than Google. We can keep that in mind for our target audience. Additionally, we see that a movie called *Eagle Eye* came out in 2008 that we will likely not need to pay attention to.

**Variety Is the Spice of Life!**

Bing Webmaster Tools (*http://www.bing.com/toolbox/webmaster*) can also be used for organic keyword search. Remember that the demographics for some search engines differ from others. Perform research not just on Google but where your potential site visitors are most likely to be.

Now we will try DuckDuckGo for a fun comparison (Figure 5-2).

*Figure 5-2. Perform searches in multiple search engines to compare suggestions.*

We now know that the eagle cam is indeed popular because it has risen in search interest to the very top (since the last time we checked). Theoretically, you'll do this type of research in a few different engines or sites over a period of time. We also now know in the eyes of two search engines that an eagle is considered an animal, a band, a thriller starring Shia LaBeouf, and a company that makes travel gear.

Since we're starting an eagle conservation site, we'll need to think about how *any* of these buckets (areas) can help us. We need to think about what information does not make sense. For example, sorry not sorry to the late 90s Swedish rocker, Eagle-Eye Cherry, you're not joining this keyword party. *Maybe if I'd typed in the hyphen…*

The most likely keyword candidate to consider studying the surrounding data of is the eagle cam (*http://www.dceaglecam.org*). We can now safely study the eagle cam site based in Washington, DC, because this project also aims to increase awareness of conservation for the majestic national bird of the United States. In truth, there are at least 16 countries (*https://en.wikipedia.org/wiki/List_of_national_birds*) across the globe that name a various species of the eagle as their national bird.

Once the rough buckets and keyword goals are defined, no matter how loosely, the next phase of *search* research starts. Tools like Moz's Keyword Explorer (*https://moz.com/tools/keyword-difficulty*), Wordtracker (*https://app.wordtracker.com*), SEM-rush (*https://www.semrush.com*), SpyFu (*http://www.spyfu.com*), Google Trends (*https://www.google.com/trends*), or Keyword Planner (*https://adwords.google.com/KeywordPlanner*) are typically the next step when performing keyword research.

Take your query or list of queries and let the games begin! If the bucket of search is enormous, then find a data fork in the road to take or try a trends tool *first*. Keyword research should be a creative and analytical enterprise. Make your best guesses when thinking of different phrasing; chances are you'll be somewhat right and wrong at the same time. I've found that the keyword combination is typically what the site owner thinks people search balanced with actual trends in search. It's also OK and quite efficient to throw paid search into the mix for experiments. All learning about the user, search queries, etc. will help. Think of keywords like races: which term or phrase is going to get you in front of the right person?

I like to make queries compete in the markets I'm targeting to see who comes out the victor. First I select my category (Figure 5-3).

*Figure 5-3. The breakdown listed in the Google Trends search window is useful information to file away for later.*

After selecting the bird category, things get interesting. When devising a site's key-word topology, categorization is especially meaningful to an SEO. Once you have a rough impression in your mind of the search landscape for keywords, it's a good idea to start looking at other tools, like Google Trends (*https://www.google.com/trends*) research (Figure 5-4).

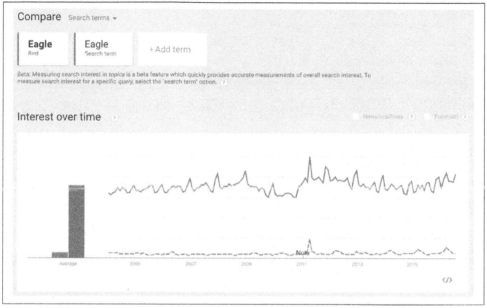

*Figure 5-4. We get a better idea of how small search interest is overall for the bird versus the search term.*

We can see in Figure 5-4 that this new categorization is a beta feature. New features are rolled out all of the time—it's important to take note of that. By way of the related searches pane at the bottom, we start to get more ideas. We're also tipped off about something we hadn't considered previously after selecting the Rising tab on the bottom right (Figure 5-5).

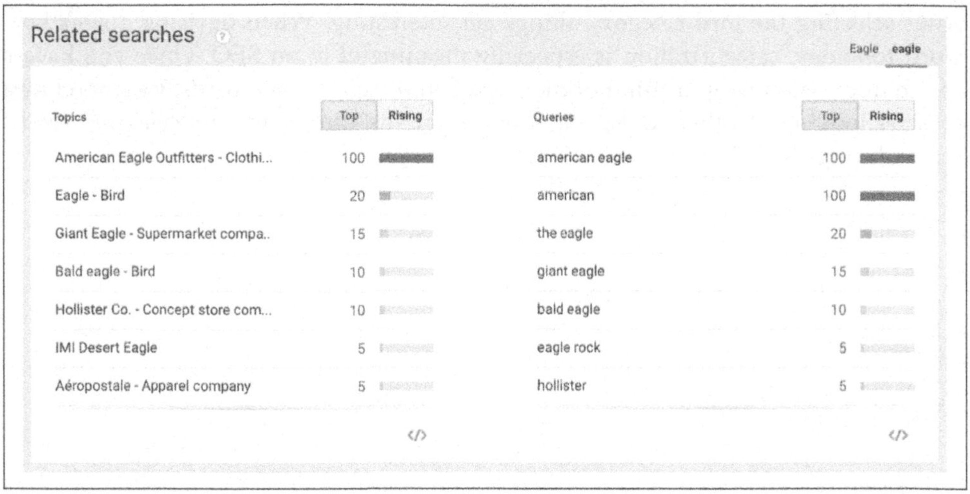

**Related searches**

Eagle | **eagle**

| Topics | Top | Rising | | Queries | Top | Rising |
|---|---|---|---|---|---|---|
| American Eagle Outfitters - Clothi... | 100 | | | american eagle | 100 | |
| Eagle - Bird | 20 | | | american | 100 | |
| Giant Eagle - Supermarket compa.. | 15 | | | the eagle | 20 | |
| Bald eagle - Bird | 10 | | | giant eagle | 15 | |
| Hollister Co. - Concept store com... | 10 | | | bald eagle | 10 | |
| IMI Desert Eagle | 5 | | | eagle rock | 5 | |
| Aéropostale - Apparel company | 5 | | | hollister | 5 | |

*Figure 5-5. Hey, wait! There's a store named American Eagle that's possibly on the rise that we should watch out for. We do not want to rank for "American Eagle" or compete there.*

Let's take a look at the organic interest for bald eagles and examine whether or not it's on the rise categorically (Figure 5-6).

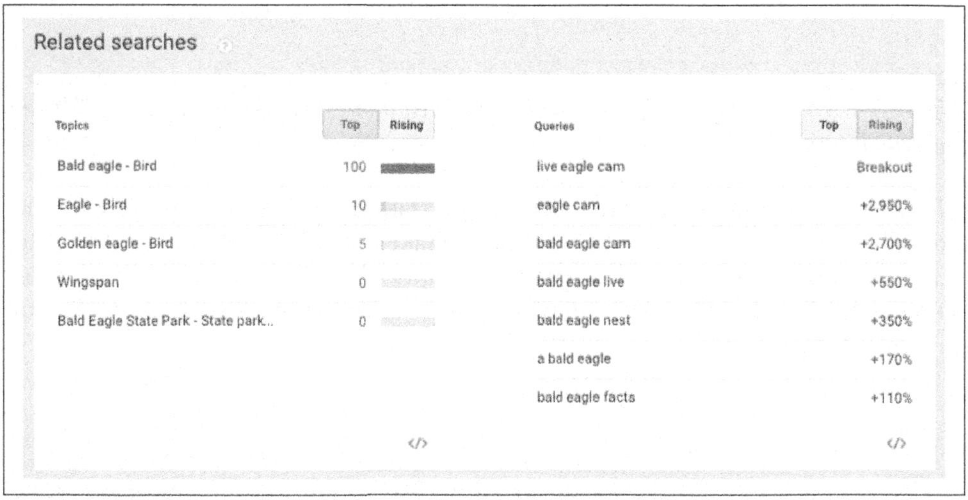

**Related searches**

| Topics | Top | Rising | | Queries | Top | Rising |
|---|---|---|---|---|---|---|
| Bald eagle - Bird | 100 | | | live eagle cam | | Breakout |
| Eagle - Bird | 10 | | | eagle cam | | +2,950% |
| Golden eagle - Bird | 5 | | | bald eagle cam | | +2,700% |
| Wingspan | 0 | | | bald eagle live | | +550% |
| Bald Eagle State Park - State park... | 0 | | | bald eagle nest | | +350% |
| | | | | a bald eagle | | +170% |
| | | | | bald eagle facts | | +110% |

*Figure 5-6. Huzzah, we see a suggestion that the eagle cam is on the rise!*

Now we understand what surrounds "eagle" as a search term. We're starting to run out of useful ideas since we are seeing so many unrelated search terms. Time to start looking elsewhere. It's not a bad idea to also use Google's PPC Keyword Planner (*https://adwords.google.com/KeywordPlanner*) tool to generate lists of new keyword ideas (Figure 5-7). You'll get to see what competition looks like as well.

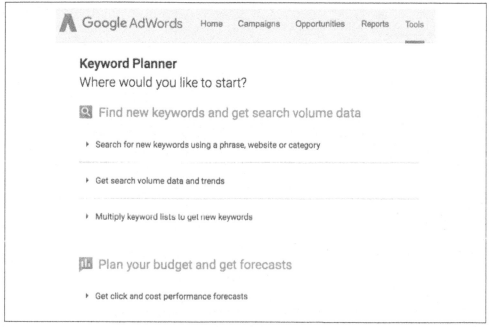

*Figure 5-7. Generally, you'll want to start with at least a few variations to get suggested keywords.*

Once you have your list, it's easy to examine the keyword interest. In this case I've chosen "bald eagle" to try and eliminate some of the noise. I do not want to rank for "American eagle" or "eagle cam." The query has some interest, but it also looks like interest has dropped recently (Figure 5-8). This type of spike indicates a news spike of some type where interest was high and then trailed off.

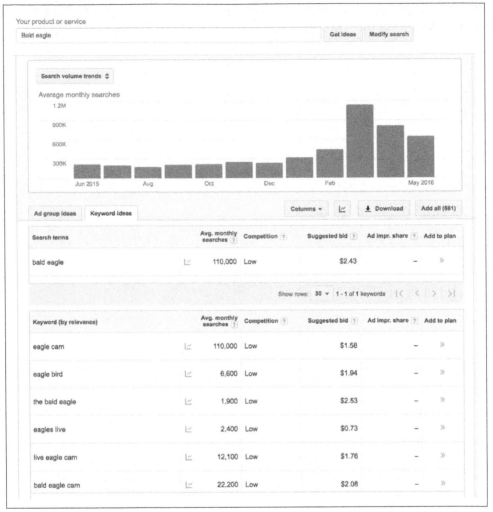

*Figure 5-8. Based on timing and news, people searching for "bald eagle" may have been doing so just to watch the famous Washington, DC Bald Eagle Cam (http://www.dceagle cam.org).*

At this point, I like to export the lists from both tools and then cross-compare. If there's a set of keywords that will then appear on both lists, you've likely got a winner. Winning terms for the example just given would be useful for marketing the bald eagle cam. If you were looking to rank for eagle-shaped teacups and mugs, then you'd need to try another approach.

Search isn't always going to be in the web browser; it's everywhere there's connectivity and devices. Cast the net wide in the beginning and whittle down the keyword targets as you go based on performance.

# Showtime! Check All Systems

So you've got some rough keyword targets (buckets) locked down. Nice job. Now we will do one more check by digging into the site's source. You have to know what you're dealing with before you can determine where to go. Keywords were once the ultimate goal of the SEO, but as our technology landscape has grown, so have our battlefields. It's most important to focus on increasing overall traffic from organic search, not on specific target keywords per se.

 If ecommerce conversions are already present in analytics or there's use of a shopping cart, it's always best to correlate them to a secondary data source regularly.

How do we put the program into practice, you may be wondering. There's one final and very critical piece to set up, the physical site audit. Now that we have our keyword targets and search goals, we can begin examining the physical website audit:

- Review the source of the site to see how it's put together. What CMS do they use?
- Data capture integrity check. Understand where the various tracking scripts lie and if any customization has happened.
- Check for abandoned tools or scripts no longer in use and commented-out code.
- Check the physical size of the images on the site.
- Test all offers (i.e., webforms) on any page where the form or content is unique.
- Use a utility to check for broken links.
- Physically click around on the links in the site to get a sense for how the funnel works.
- Review site speed performance. Ascertain how many servers are being called.
- It's also important to check the page for W3C validation (*https://valida tor.w3.org/*) and do timing tests (*https://developers.google.com/speed/pagespeed/ insights/*).

When starting a program, I like to take screenshots of the website and social media accounts and annotate before any work is performed. It's also a good idea to set up Google alerts on the major keyword topics. You should also activate alerts on the competition so you're passively being made aware of any big announcements or press coverage.

If proper analytics tools are *not* deployed for some reason, correct that horrific error and then take it day by day. In analytics, begin to study which traffic sources are bringing *the most* traffic and balance your future efforts with which sources *perform the best*. Performance can be judged by time spent on a site, number of pages reviewed, or conversions themselves. It's a marketer's dream to be able to calculate conversion costs. This dream can become reality! Set up analytics, create benchmarks, and deploy any other tools.

Regardless of what types of analytics and tools you use, there are many free ones available. Google Analytics (GA) is free and the tracking script is easy to deploy, but do not forget Google Webmaster Tools (GMT). It's crucial to combine GA with GMT for website SEO. Creating benchmarks within analytics can be as simple as an annotation in GA denoting when the program is beginning. Documentation is the key to understanding where you've started. Memories get fuzzy and site management changes hands so annotations are the key to making meaningful observations.

Once you've checked what's behind the scenes, you can perform the SEO audit on-page. The on-page audit involves a deep eyeballing of the page. Take a good look at the page and compare it against any data you have on the effectiveness of links. For example, when looking at the homepage, you can see in most analytics tools where people are clicking from that page. If something seems askew, like a web form that's hard to read or too far below the fold, then chances are it's not working well.

In the early days, we saw users creating a boomerang pattern with their eye patterns in the heat maps. Jakob Nielsen (*http://bit.ly/2n6yQuw*)'s research shows that it's more like an F (*https://en.wikipedia.org/wiki/Screen_reading*) pattern in the current age (Figure 5-9).

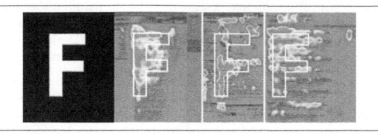

*Figure 5-9. Using Neuroscience to Design a Better Blog (https://blog.kissmetrics.com/ using-neuroscience-for-blogs) (Source: Kissmetrics).*

Content is the current vehicle for keyword expansion in search. That could change at any time. It's a historical misconception that one can simply "power it out" by *stuffing keywords* into every nook and cranny. Think back to the days of the research paper and seek to build credibility page by page for the corresponding keyword.

Keywords are no longer the endgame of SEO; they are more of a guiding light. I have seen many folks in the industry decry keywords as becoming less important than before. Keywords were once one of the most definitive ways for us to measure SEO progress, but this has changed as our measurement tools have improved.

Jayson Demers, who writes about SEO for Forbes (*http://www.forbes.com*), has said that keywords still do matter.

> To put it simply, keywords do still matter in 2016. Chances are they'll always matter, to an extent. However, as search engines have become more sophisticated, they have started putting far less emphasis on specific keywords, and more emphasis on the meaning or intent behind those keywords.

*Context matters* more than it ever has to search. Context is best determined by intent. It used to be good enough to harvest the intent of a search, but that's not longer true. Now it's important to *generate* intention as well as harvest it. Perhaps the better way to think about it is not just as keywords, but as intent *signaled*.

---

## Getting Traffic

Use keywords thoughtfully, but don't be spammy about it. The growth in traffic will not come from just placing keyboards everywhere. In the beginning, it's OK to leverage other platforms in your programs for traffic. Eventually it's necessary to build your own organic program no matter what, though—you have to diversify. For example, if you leverage a weekly trending topic on Twitter for boosts of traffic, then you have to be aware that if the company goes under or gets sold, you're toast.

---

# Competitors

Everything we put out on the web is fairly transparent: websites, social media, and content distribution are all public information. Study your competitors early and often, and set up auto alerts for web mentions of their names. The benefits of learning from other people's strategies and online marketing spend are countless.

You can safely sign up for a competitor's offers on their site to test them. I sometimes test competitors by clicking on their paid search ads as well, but do not recommend doing this excessively (it's uncool).

My first step in looking at competitors is to plainly view what they put out there and then categorize it. Simply review the competition's source and social media. Reading a website's meta title and description will allow you to uncover the targets of their marketing program. If they also happen to list their meta keywords in the source, that's even better. You can also view what tracking tools they're using. In hyper-competitive markets, knowing the subtle differences in tools, styles, and even hosts can make a difference.

It's advantageous to gain knowledge from the investments of others in their SEO. There are tools to study what other sites are using for PPC. Otherwise it's easy to review a competitor's website source and glean all sorts of information. Start a spreadsheet and begin gathering the crucial information. Any meta keywords listed will tell you what targets the competition thinks are important. Social media listings and descriptions should be pulled into the same spreadsheet for analysis.

# Reporting

The reporting of a search marketing program can sometimes *make or break* the program. It is also an area where I have seen many people spend excessive amounts of time. If you are struggling with reporting, that generally means the goals are unclear —or even worse—and that performance levels are not good.

People become most skeptical about SEO when they don't understand what they're getting; reporting is where everything gets cleared up.

Where I've seen programs fail is by staying *too insular* with what's going on. If you're doing the work and things are improving, then showing data should be an easy thing to do. If you're skating by or have mediocre numbers, then reporting is always going to induce agony.

As already mentioned, it's most important to pick a few key metrics and report on them consistently. Do not change metrics suddenly or cherry-pick data sets, which can sometimes border on dishonesty.

Here are a few sample metrics to report month-over-month (MOM) for a site:

- CTR for all traffic sources (aka value of traffic)
- Unique page visits/pageviews via all traffic sources
- Unbranded keyword visits to the site
- Quality and number of backlinks to the site
- Page engagement: bounce rate, session duration
- Social shares and corresponding site traffic from social (by channel)

Metrics reported on should directly correspond to the marketing activities happening. If you are only reporting and not doing any of the work, the above metrics are a good way to start. My preferred way to pull together information is with a dashboard. Most tools have some type of prebuilt or suggested reports. The tool I often pull together reports in is Google Analytics (Figure 5-10), but there are other tools as well.

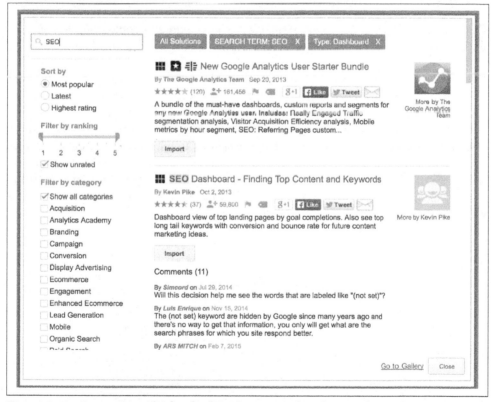

*Figure 5-10. Over 700 results for the "SEO" query within the Google Analytics Solutions Gallery. So many places to start!*

To create a dashboard, simply select one from the Google Analytics Solutions gallery. Read reviews and choose the one that fits what you need. Click on Reporting then on Dashboards → +New Dashboard (Figure 5-11).

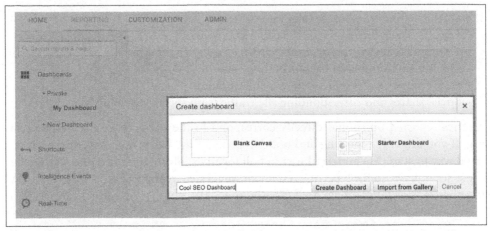

*Figure 5-11. Creating a "cool" SEO dashboard gives you an at-a-glance snapshot of important data.*

Deciding what matters to your program should be governed by how you spend your time. Are you running social for the site? Then definitely include a widget about social. My recommendation for what to choose in a dashboard always starts from what the key stakeholders want to see. Some people, for example, really care about raw traffic numbers; it's an indicator of success to them. Others prefer straight-up conversions or final sales. It's always good to build one widget *per activity* performed, so if we're running social, email, and PPC as services, I'd show at-a-glance information for each area respectively. In the case of the dashboard snippet in Figure 5-12, we were running both content and social programs for SEO.

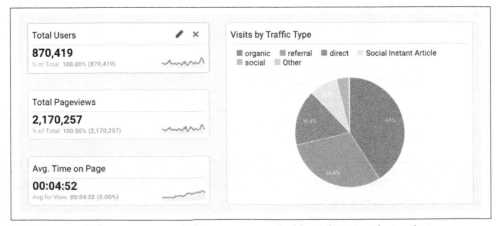

*Figure 5-12. An example snippet from a content dashboard in Google Analytics.*

If we want to drill down more specifically on social media, we should be studying the data within the platforms themselves as well as how those users interact with the site (Figure 5-13).

| Traffic from Social Networks | | |
|---|---|---|
| Social Network | Sessions | Bounce Rate |
| Facebook | 155,582 | 62.29% |
| reddit | 111,557 | 54.77% |
| Twitter | 78,404 | 61.19% |
| LinkedIn | 4,680 | 65.53% |
| Google+ | 822 | 52.07% |
| Techmeme | 571 | 73.20% |
| Pocket | 432 | 50.46% |
| Hacker News | 429 | 58.04% |
| Disqus | 332 | 46.08% |
| Naver | 286 | 57.34% |

| Social Visits & Quality from Mobile | | |
|---|---|---|
| Mobile Device Info | Sessions | Avg. Time on Page |
| Apple iPhone | 32,127 | 00:06:39 |
| Apple iPad | 10,975 | 00:05:45 |
| Apple iPhone 6 | 3,201 | 00:09:39 |
| (not set) | 2,521 | 00:06:04 |
| Samsung SM-G935F Galaxy S7 Edge | 2,454 | 00:05:01 |
| Apple iPhone 6s | 2,443 | 00:04:23 |
| Samsung SM-G920F Galaxy S6 | 2,429 | 00:05:25 |
| Samsung SM-G930F Galaxy S7 | 1,876 | 00:05:24 |
| Google Nexus 6P | 1,709 | 00:05:41 |
| Apple iPad Air 2 | 1,498 | 00:07:42 |

*Figure 5-13. Traffic and mobile quality from social media.*

We know that social media activity happens quite frequently on mobile, it's the easiest way to share and digest information. Nearly 80% (*http://mklnd.com/2nvV61X*) of overall time spent on social is on mobile.

What is the price of a super sweet tweet? It depends. Ecommerce sites have the clearer path to conversion over those who do not. An organization must carve out what they deem a lead's worth to be, which typically depends on deal size and how long it takes to close. In Figure 5-14 you'll find an example of a signature verified dashboard (by use of initials and dates in the headings).

The dashboard in Figure 5-14 helps us to see that our conversion rate is OK. We also know our best sales days are typically Wednesday to Friday and that Google organic is our biggest verified method of search input. Clearly, we have some data capture issues to resolve in the GA account shown in Figure 5-14, because we never want to see such a high percentage of direct/none as a traffic referral.

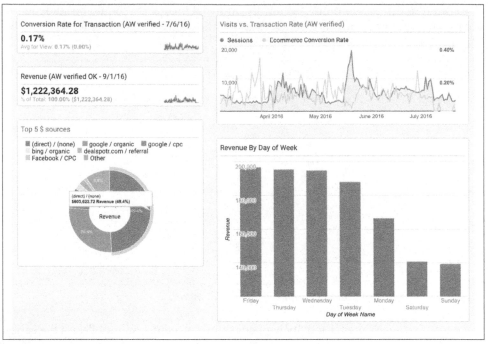

*Figure 5-14. Note that this ecommerce dashboard has verified information with initials and dates for easy reference.*

### Not All Widgets Work

Sometimes, depending on how your goals are mapped out in Google Analytics, you won't get an exact match for conversions you are expecting to see. I have seen dashboards report data differently than the Goals section sometimes. I do not know why this happens, but sometimes when you use filters or other more intricate tools you'll have to take an extra step.

Many lovable widgets are available in the Google Analytics Solutions gallery. It will take some energy to customize the dashboard if you decide to go prebuilt. Also, note that nobody else can see your dashboard in Google Analytics unless you specifically share it with others (Figure 5-15).

*Figure 5-15. Select Share Object for others with GA access to see what you've built. Share in the gallery if your dashboard is so freaking cool you cannot keep it for yourself.*

It's also extremely useful to review dashboards with a date comparison range. Measurement over time for the same metrics is a sure road to realization when coupled with annotations. If everyone involved in the SEO program agrees that your dashboard reflects what's important, then you can also run month-over-month (MOM) analysis for those metrics in an automated fashion.

I like to compare a month or more of data to a previous period. Typically it's fine to compare one month versus the previous month, except for the summer months. In seasonal industries, it's very typical to see a drop-off in traffic for the summer or during the heart of winter. When comparing data sets for a seasonal company, it's most useful to look at the same period the previous year to better gauge performance (Figure 5-16).

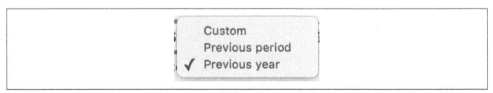

*Figure 5-16. In the date selection panel of GA in the top right when viewing any data, comparisons are available.*

## Branding Matters

When reporting on value, it's important to separate branded search terms from non-branded ones. Unless there are specific concerns and needs, effort should not go into ranking for brand. Nonbranded keyword terms are the ones SEOs can definitely view as a product of their efforts.

Many companies stuff their name into the beginning of the title attribute of a page, but ranking for the name is the easiest thing to do. Instead, focus on what's relevant to the page itself.

By now, you've picked some program goals, built consensus, checked under the hood, started keyword bucket identification, and figured out how to pull together a GA dashboard. You trust your data and have checked for all the basics to ensure site health.

The next phase for the search program is to start embarking on your outbound campaigns like social media content sharing, creating content, and beyond. Huzzah!

# CHAPTER 6

# Campaign Management

Campaigns are a coordinated marketing effort amongst different mediums to promote a product, message, or service. A campaign that runs without a target or goal is not a campaign; it's just marketing activity, which may be OK. My larger point is that these are separate enterprises. While SEO tends to be a more long-term play, it is entirely possible to do a campaign in the short term that will cross-pollinate through to SEO efforts.

Without campaigns, there is no start nor finish to any major marketing event. Specific goals and timeframes can help to galvanize stakeholders and coalesce teams. Just as we sometimes feel more inspired when there's a push, it also gives us an end to look forward to where we can reset, look at the accumulated data, and evaluate metrics.

## Campaign SEO Juice

When done correctly, campaigns help boost traffic, user engagement, awareness, and therefore search prominence of a site. The goals tend to vary, but typical ones are branding, launching a new product, or cultivating new business from existing customers. Campaigns can be short or long, but the thread tying it all together is *always* the overarching goal. A campaign without a goal is like a warrior without a battle ahead.

Some organic search efforts are viewed as a failure because of the sheer amount of time it can take to to see statistically significant results. This is especially true in established long-running SEO programs. Campaigns actually help SEO politically as well as technically. By picking select targets and getting those target goals refined, you can start to achieve results in a way non-SEOs understand. A battle many SEOs must fight is gaining consensus that their activities are fruitful (i.e., is this stuff working?).

When a campaign is pulled off correctly, it enhances a company's organic efforts. The correlation between SEO and campaigns does not feel like a direct one, but a logical connection does exist. To go out and crusade for traffic can feel as though you're the only one gaining visits to your site or seeing assets that are being promoted. However, the more users *enjoy* the content on your site, the higher the visibility and relevancy. Everything we do on the web is tracked. Every handshake is culled for information. What's relevant to humans will eventually interest the other aforementioned creatures of the internet—crawlers, spiders, etc. Interesting traffic garners more traffic in a way that corresponds to Benjamin Franklin's "Magic of Compound Interest" (*http://bit.ly/ 2mfr68F*).

Performing SEO by campaign is not a classical (i.e., *historical*) mode of thinking; it is perhaps more akin to twin growth hacking. However, it's opportune to have both short- and long-term goals with any given search program. Campaigns can sometimes be like an off-road reconnaissance mission: you're putting things out beyond the safety of the homepage, resulting in valuable traffic and data from different sources, aka signals.

Viral campaigns are the golden chalice to every marketer. Just like winning an Oscar, they are the gold standard for proof of success. No viral video or asset I've ever seen (for commercial purposes) happens without the assistance of a coordinated campaign. The type of campaigns classified as "grassroots" or "guerrilla" tend to involve risks. It can be difficult to demand attention without evoking some type of emotion, so remember to make sure your risk exposure does not exceed your risk appetite. Unoffensive risks are best; follow what you were taught about the dinner table with guests—no politics, no religion, etc. Sometimes comedy can allow for hilarity in tone that will elicit a response, but tread carefully. Anthropology and sociology are interesting areas to study if you want to understand what compels a group of people to become offended or endeared.

---

## Campaign Hesitation?

If you're devising a campaign that doesn't feel right, consider sleeping on it. *Delay the launch.* Everyone can wait one more day for your offer. If you sleep on it and do not hit send on a campaign, you can reconsider the next day. Post-slumber, it may only take a hot second to figure out what about it is still bothering you. Shower ideas are *real*. With fresh morning eyes, if your campaign still seems like a good one, huzzah! Go for it!

If you're still struggling with your campaign after a night's rest, phone a colleague. Send the creatives to someone who can give an honest opinion, preferably under NDA (by the way I am *so* not a lawyer and cannot give advice in this realm).

Remember, just because something may reach the height of hilarity does not necessarily mean by itself that the consumer will get out their wallet. A more conservative

---

> stance to endorse could be the *grandma rule*: do not send out anything publicly that your elder relatives wouldn't like.

The goal of search is to get content in front of the right people at the time they are looking for it. Successful campaigns lead to notoriety you wouldn't otherwise get by just hanging about. A focused light always brings the most heat. One of my mentors once taught me to always *be the laser*, not the flashlight. At the data level, strive for as much accuracy as possible. At the high level, your goal is to weave these data sources into a rich tapestry of information. Don't get distracted by one-offs. While others are fighting about whether to use a flashlight or a laser focus, your goal is to turn on the lights in the room when all the elements line up correctly. Shine the brightest wherever you can online with all the sources you have at your disposal; campaigns are designed to do this masterfully.

# Mobile Campaign

The best campaigns vary by location, target, and budget, but one tenet remains constant: use what you've got. Combined forces give you more strength. If you have a landing page template ready to go, an idea, and an email list, then run with those together. You might be tempted to keep an ace or two in your back pocket like an Old West poker player, but for continuous success you want to design a *system*, not "cowboy it up" every time.

Don't end up with a bullet in your back. But that doesn't mean you can't be imaginative. There are so many amazing and free services available these days that you can construct a campaign without breaking the bank. Your wildest imagination coupled with a harness to the real world will produce the strongest campaigns. This chapter will cover some different types of campaigns that, when done right, can provide great wealth, eternal youth, or probably just traffic and SEO benefits.

Banner ads and in-app purchases were the first way advertisers were able to reach users on mobile. Click rates, however, were about as abysmal as you'd expect. It's hard to say equivocally that banner advertising is dead, but it's not something a client has asked for in at least five years. We know people are spending significant time on their phones, so do not interrupt—try to add to their day. Make someone feel better or solve a problem. Mobile campaigns that seek to jump in front of the user with no value will get left behind by the user.

The proliferation of mobile phones in our lives means local geo-campaigns are super en vogue for advertisers. There are also some organic components to mobile SEO such as the NAP (see "Local Search" on page 128), good usability, etc. There are a few campaigns that need to tie heavily into local search to truly work, such as location-based campaigns like scavenger hunts, geocaching, and contests.

We have increased capabilities (opportunities) on mobile to engage with people, from location to camera to gyroscope. Tablets have touch experiences that can transform user experiences immensely. Typically a responsive mobile landing page or website is all that's needed as an asset for a directed offer campaign on mobile. There's little reason to create an app for campaign purposes unless it is to elicit money for app purchases, sharing of content, or another well-defined business goal. A top-performing mobile page will suffice to help direct email into traffic.

We have only begun to skim the surface of augmented reality (AR) and virtual reality (VR) marketing campaign integrations with too many industries to count at this point.

# Email Marketing

Whether it's a webinar or a landing page, email moves the needle when done right. Email is not the most exciting type of campaign, but it can be the least expensive to produce. Experimentation can be done with so many tiny elements, like the size of the subject line, that it can seem silly. There are higher email open rates when your subject is shorter, but readers tend to click more on emails with longer subjects. There are no limits to experimentation with this type of campaign. The amount of time an email is opened versus the clicks it receives is but one metric to consider when measuring an email campaign.

Perhaps some adorable baby eagles are about to hatch, and you want people to find it on mobile. Think about what you have to offer in your email campaign. Is it a freebie or are you asking people to pay for a preview of an eagle cam?

What's old is new again with email. I fondly recall the LISTSERV! Email was the first killer app of the internet, but it was surpassed by the World Wide Web long ago. Or was it? Even the nontechnical and the elderly understand email—even seven-year-olds understand email. It's not just spam: it's newsletters, coupons, and all kinds of updates. These are the children of the "community newsletter" or "'zines."

The content is already there. The users are already there. It's some of the *most* targeted audience out there. So you don't purchase the mailing list, you purchase space in the newsletter. The user can click on these and get sent to your product. They don't even have to maintain an infrastructure, they just use someone else's (like mailgun (*http://www.mailgun.com*)). The advertisers, however, still have to maintain a website; otherwise, there will be nothing to click through to! You could start your own newsletter, but unless you're committed to original content on a consistent basis, *don't*. You're just creating spam, and you won't get a very good retention *or* click-through rate.

The real value of these newsletters is that people trust them because they have used them for months or years, much longer than the duration of the usual web campaign.

Of course, once you obtain that level of trust, the next level is the old "form letter." Fast-forward to today, and this translates to a unique message sent "only to you," updated with your likes or dislikes. Maybe only people interested in yellow pool toys got this message. Maybe people who liked any kind of pool toy got a different message or no message at all.

---

## Example Mobile Email Campaign

The following are some steps for how to run a renegade email campaign with mobile in mind:

1. Collect emails from customers and prospects during all marketing activities such as trade shows, happy hours, and any website(s).
2. Establish a weekly mobile-friendly email with updates, news, coupons, or loyalty programs. Make sure the email contains information that conveys the perception of value. Classic examples would be a coupon code or some tangible reward like access to exclusive events and information.
3. Gain readership by aggregating data. Start including links within the emails to website blog content (surrounding the business) and include community information where relevant.
4. Include mobile-friendly links as the call to action (CTA) for users, which could prompt for further user activity like an app install or sharing the content on social.

---

Years ago, I coined a term to explain our *attraction* to offers and the feeling we need to create in order to get a response to landing pages (or anything with an offer). I call this *the Velvet Rope* (see Figure 6-1). There are two types of people, those who wait in lines and those who will do anything to jump them. It became clearer to me that the more exclusive an offer is, the more *excited* people feel about it. Waiting in line doesn't feel good, but skipping the line does. Campaigns that have a *virtual* velvet rope make people feel special because they are part of a chosen few.

It's difficult to convey exclusivity in an offer that's made to everyone without appearing transparent. It helps to have specific dates with the offer, meaning that if it's running for *one month only*, then say as much.

An exclusivity-style campaign works best with email or social media. You're looking for people who already have some type of peripheral relationship or familiarity with you. You have to compel them to want to wait in line or give them a way to feel like they're jumping the line.

*Figure 6-1. The Velvet Rope makes offers feel more exclusive and therefore more exciting*

In an old campaign, we offered three devices from a new product line our client was about to put out on a popular crowdfunding site. These were cool gadgets nobody could get yet, but everyone wanted them. We had a segmented email list so we were able to identify who had signed up for email (and when), who was mostly opening those emails, and who had visited the site from said emails. We sent messages to the loyal visitors thanking them for their interest and offered the coveted device to the first responders by a certain date chosen at random. They had to fill out a quick form with two choices: to opt in to communications by the company and future product announcements (via a newsletter).

### Consent Matters!

It doesn't feel exclusive to *anyone* to hit a site and then get spammed immediately afterwards, especially if they have not signed up for email or any other offers. Asking for the opt-in is always worth the extra step because overall adoption rates are lower but click-throughs *are higher*.

The numbers feel lower when you ask for opt-ins, but the response is *so much stronger* that it's always worth it. Do not place a high value on the number of subscribers in an email list, but rather ongoing trends. Are you getting *more* unsubscribes and spam reports each month or *less*?

## Social Campaigns

Social fire has a way of making online things light up. Many companies create videos in hopes of making them viral from the outset, but that's not really how it works.

Every overnight success takes vast networks and channels to promote the content: it's not just Reddit. If the social media campaign is thoroughly planned out and targeted to the right folks, a campaign will generally outperform more traditional marketing practices like direct mail and press releases.

Leverage built-in product features to get existing users to share the experience with new users. Cleverly integrating social sharing into post-sales only stands to benefit a company. Dropbox once gave away huge chunks of free storage in return for referrals, which helped them grow virally. Twitter noticed that users without followers in the first use of the platform seldom came back, so they curated choices for people to follow their interests.

Cross-posting across social media platforms is great when done correctly, however each platform needs a tailored approach. I would not share a picture of someone on a beach or at a bar if it was LinkedIn unless the company was selling vacations.

Real-time audience interaction is what makes social so fun. We're seeing more and more publishers leverage Facebook Live's (*https://live.fb.com*) capabilities because people can interact with friends, celebrities with fans, and the like. Periscope (*https://www.periscope.tv*) has made it easy to connect quickly with people who follow you. It's not uncommon to see social media sites appearing more and more in the top of the SERPs.

---

### Social Campaign Tips

Social and SEO are like peanut butter and jelly. Put them together thoughtfully and reap rewards; here are a few tips:

- Use tracking URLs from your analytics suite, not just the tool you use for posting.
- Do not auto-post during a live event; it can get weird if the schedule slides a bit or unplanned events like inclement weather happen.
- Don't pick a Twitter hashtag that is more than 14 characters, 10% of the total Tweet limit.
- Consider like-gating or action-gating to get what you want from the user.
- Maintain and build your list of contacts from social; they can be used to target ads or future promotions.
- If you're worried about how something *feels* to your audience, then read those posts aloud before sending them out; it helps makes them more human.

---

# Content Campaigns

When crafting content, it's more important for it to make sense to the reader than for it to contain a bunch of keywords. The Google quality guidelines (*http://bit.ly/*

*2lPErB5*) use an analogy I find a little funny but sweet, *E-A-T*: expertise, authoritativeness, and trustworthiness. Focus on creating compelling content. Always ask yourself, "Why on earth should they care about what I want them to?"

Blogs in the form of lists (i.e., listicles) do amazingly well as articles because people know what they're getting. One can trust that the listicle will give them a TL;DR perspective of an article; it's supposed to be an outline. TL;DR was very popular for a little while as a way to say, if you're thinking this is *too long, don't read*, then here's all you need to know in a concise sentence or two. For example:

TL;DR: the steppe eagle (Figure 6-2) enjoys a majestic stature and plumage, which is notably dark brown.

*Figure 6-2. Our steppe eagle (http://econews.am/?p=5915&l=en) friend is just hanging out, so effortlessly cool.*

It was popular for a while to include a "*TL;DR: insert summary here*" at the top of an article to build user interest in a post. I could not find definitive statistics on how much the inclusion of said *acronym and synopsis* helped build trust. I *do* know from many years of experience that giving users what you are actually promising invariably reaps rewards. Retargeting is the subtle way to track people who've visited your site for a paid infusion of traffic. Sending out emails with recaps of blog posts, events, and sweet Tweets are always solid campaigns. If people are interested in what you're doing, they're likely to talk to you, so keep it real.

One campaign to coordinate boosting traffic bumps is sending out email to remind people within an organization to share content at coordinated times. It helps to also do external content creation like guest posting on Medium, LinkedIn Pulse, or other sites that allow guest contributions. Link to others when it makes sense from your content; this will help the engines categorize you.

Content does really well when it's regularly created and promoted—if people are interested, of course! One of the reasons I believe that trending topics on Twitter happen is the regularity. Content can have the same effect with a group of opted-in followers. Over the years I have followed a myriad of companies' email lists who simply did a good job of keeping me informed on things I wanted to know. Weekly recaps of top stories and content that's useful to the person getting it can move mountains for a company.

Content also lies at the heart of SEO, so it's not a horrible idea to post emails to the site if the content is new. Many companies have dozens of PDFs with rich product information that do not have consistent titling or meta descriptions, which are a good idea for branding alone. For a long time, we've been able to embed some extra information in PDF assets; it only takes a few minutes.

Typical digital content campaigns I've worked on often include the following mediums: landing pages or microsites tied to email, organic social, and paid social. It is considered a little more experimental by some to use social for traffic, but not as much as social bookmarking. Using Reddit to push out a press hit is definitely experimental, but some element of spice must be present to get a spark.

# Crowdfunding Campaigns

Another great way to generate revenue for a site is to simply *ask for it*. The Maker Movement (*http://makerfaire.com/maker-movement*) has inspired thousands of entrepreneurs to boldly go forth and create incredible new products and services. Millions of dollars (*http://bit.ly/2n6E8pV*) have been raised via crowdfunding to support the efforts on these sites. People have also been using Kiva (*https://www.kiva.org*) for over ten years to perform microlending on an international scale.

Launching a campaign to boost a crowdfunding campaign takes a lot of muscle. When done correctly, the rewards are monumental. Some of the most popular crowdfunding sites at the time of writing are GoFundMe (*https://www.gofundme.com*), IndieGoGo (*https://www.indiegogo.com*), and Kickstarter (*https://www.kickstarter.com*) (in no particular order). These crowdfunding sites have their own *built-in audiences*, but coordinated efforts can also be used to boost rankings. There have been a number of famous crowdfunding campaigns, but one of the most controversial (and viral) was for potato salad (*http://kck.st/2nNHQSz*) by Zach "Danger" Brown, who raised more than $50,000. LeVar Burton's Reading Rainbow

Kickstarter was also a very interesting campaign and raised a significant amount of literacy awareness and money (*http://kck.st/2lVbPHr*) for an important cause.

The most winning combination that I've used for crowdfunding success combines offline and online, social and paid. The common denominator between all activities should be hustle.

---

## Example Campaign

Every business wants to raise money quickly when they have a hot idea or new product to promote. I've worked on some hugely successful crowdfunding campaigns. The following are some tips from those experiences:

- Start talking to people you know; they will be the most motivated to help you. Just like selling knives door to door, a random stranger is less motivated to open the door to buy a knife than your mom is. It also generally helps to offer something before asking for something, like the classic offer of free pizza for helping someone move.
  — Throw parties.
  — Have lunches.
  — Pick up the phone and tell people what you're doing.
- Live events can catapult social if you own it and go full Tweet cover. People have gone viral simply by tweeting what they're overhearing on airplanes. Some folks might consider this super rude. Hijacking events doesn't mean being rude at events. There are ways to gain attention without having to host. Go to relevant conferences or meetups, attend them virtually if possible, or just participate in their Twitter hashtag discussion. Join the virtual conversation while taking part in the real-life conversation. Schedule the things you can ahead of time.
  — Sponsor or cosponsor events that are relevant to your campaign audience.
  — Host an event and list it on all locally relevant business sites.
- Use any and all email contact lists for Facebook dark ads.
- Places social ads targeted to friends of friends or people in a tight geological area.
- Coordinate a Product Hunt (*https://www.producthunt.com*) launch that is timed with the release of the post. Get friends and family lined up if you have to. It's never a good idea to use a bunch of new accounts to vote on Product Hunt, as their algorithm tries to prevent this. Instead, they prefer to rely on the community.
- Identify relevant influencers.
  — Outreach to individuals to invite them to participate.
  — Deploy targeted ads on Twitter using their handles.
  — Set up automated RSS via Twitter with a service like Twitterfeed to RT what *they* share.

---

Line up any press mentions or consider contributing guest blogs to news sites. Call upon your network for help and consider coordinating the publicity pops with sites like Reddit and Product Hunt (*https://www.producthunt.com*).

Most stuff happens in meatspace. It can be argued that most of our lives will become virtualized, but until then we have to consider that offline activity can work in conjunction with online. There's an increasing trend of growth marketers leveraging services like ring-down and outsourced call centers to give the appearance of a larger company.

### Call Center Magic

Organized effort when exerted via different mediums can have a cumulative effect. A recent new growth hacking trend has been to deploy low-cost call centers to provide services and follow-ups for potential customers. You can hire college interns or overseas vendors to create massive amounts of content. It's considered more of a mechanical approach, but it can work effectively when part of an integrated campaign.

# Growth Hacking IRL

Tying in offline rewards to online efforts reaps rich benefits. This section will cover a personal example of a guerilla marketing campaign turned into online social magic. Web forms are the transactional handshake of a website, because they contain the offer for a next step with the site. The growth hacker's duty is to find the path to the acquisition: a promise of future communication, a booked appointment, or even a final sale.

SXSW (*http://www.sxsw.com*) (South By Southwest) is a digital marketing summit in Austin, Texas put on by top internet marketers; it's their Catalina Wine Mixer (hat tip: *Step Brothers*). If you can kick off a successful campaign at the SXSW festival, then you're sure to become internet-popular. I created my most successful campaign when I experienced a problem in real life. I had a seemingly valuable asset, but the luck of the draw was mixed: renters left my Austin rental house in extremely poor condition right before SXSW Interactive.

Sometimes the best growth campaigns are born out of pure fire, drama, or chaos. I was fired up both as a landlord and also as a marketer. The challenge then became clear to me: I needed to leverage a somewhat questionable asset for *marketing* purposes at SXSW instead of money. Eureka! The solution came to me while deep in thought; I would run a contest!

It was clear to me after surveying the house that I could not charge people money to stay there, even if I did get it cleaned up in time. The cosmetic damages were extensive and the time was short. I had very little furniture, and most of it was camping gear my parents kindly contributed. My roster was already full of clients to launch that year at SXSW so I knew I didn't have time to run an Airbnb or rental situation. There was no time to throw together a bed and breakfast. Money comes with obligations (and expectations), ones I knew I couldn't meet. For three days, my friends, my parents, some TaskRabbits (*https://www.taskrabbit.com*), and I scrubbed and painted as best we could.

Quickly we put together a site with the contest rules and placed it on a bunch of social sites like Twitter, Facebook, and Reddit. My contest offer was this: *help me on some of my projects and you can stay with me for free* (Figure 6-3). It blew up (in a good way). There were too many entries to even respond to everyone.

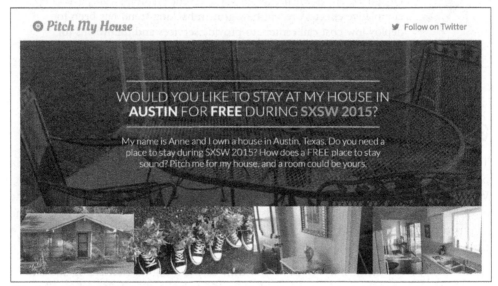

*Figure 6-3. The last year we ran the SXSW contest.*

People pitched their hearts out for a free place to stay at SXSW. Traffic jumped up overnight and we got press coverage. The winner of the contest that year was Funny or Die (*http://www.funnyordie.com*). We enjoyed some joint press coverage, thrilled all of our clients, and have been friends with Funny or Die ever since.

There is nothing wrong with a purely online campaign, but offline action is generally required for a transaction to occur. Campaigns combining offline with online experiences have the capacity to become the most powerful.

There have been a myriad of successful campaigns launching companies into the zeitgeist at SXSW and other conferences with a concentration of the right audience. Attention from a large marketing conference helps to boost a campaign, but it is not the only way. The best campaigns are those with a *strong* offer or CTA.

In the early internet marketing days, the most popular CTA used was "Click here" to evoke a user to click. Offers like "Learn More" and "Get Started" are convenient mainstays for internet marketers; these offers are so widely used that they often come with the templates themselves (not kidding). Offers become a tired concept to people when they're overused. Boring or generic offers coupled with a lack of demonstrable value will prevent people from clicking a button on any website. A strong offer will also benefit overall search prominence by boosting the click-through rate.

The website or landing page's CTA must convey value to *intrigue* the person enough so that they want to click through. Offers can vary wildly from classic to zany: get free assessments, talk to an expert, get more sleep tonight, stay awesome.

Time-based offers also perform well when the perception of value is communicated properly: an ending at a specific time or 50% off on President's Day, for example. If your offer is for an open-ended amount of time, then do not attempt to use a time-based offer. If someone returns to the site more than once and sees the same time-based offer, it will create an aura of disingenuousness. It's important to study analytics so that you can understand how well your CTAs are doing, and if they are translating into success.

> An organization's ability to learn, and translate that learning into action rapidly, is the ultimate competitive advantage.
>
> —Jack Welch, American business executive and author

Value comes directly from the perceptions of the individual on the other end of the screen. To convey value can be difficult, but it is entirely possible when you are in touch with your audience. What do they really need? Do you have it? Are you manufacturing a need or did it exist already? If so, how will you set the stage? These questions are at the heart of all marketing campaigns, be it paid or organic. If we're going to ask someone to part with their hard-earned money, always expect that they will want an explanation with regards to who, when, where, what, and why. Failing to execute on the "why" of an offer almost always results in a click away from the site.

---

## Snapchat Is Not Bric-A-Brac

Many analysts have postulated that Snapchat is the first augmented reality social network. I predict that augmented and virtual reality–based platforms will someday become one of the most popular ways we interact with marketing campaigns. Coupons will be delivered to us when we're using tilt brush or playing games.

I have seen demonstrations of virtual-reality retail experiences and they're breathtaking. Advertisers and marketers will seek to give customers a seamless online retail experience. More about the futuristic stuff later!

---

Whether your aim is guerrilla growth or the more consistent long-term type of growth, it's important to get yourself into the right mindset. If you're not the person who has creative ideas, work with someone who does. Elton John, Michael McDonald, and numerous other artists have performed some of their finest works in collaboration with others. All the stars in the sky burn just as bright. Brainstorm to find what's compelling about what you're promoting; it's there if you're looking.

You should also take a deeper look at the product you're using, or *actually* use the service you're promoting. On more occasions than I'd like to admit, I have found kinks in the flow of a new product or service. Every time we take on a new product or service at my agency, I sign up for it as a potential customer start-to-finish.

We once worked with a local moving company that was printing out all of the leads we were getting them. If the paper got lost, so did the lead. We created a simple picklist CRM for them that acted as a spreadsheet. By being able to tag and put a status or a quick note on the lead, they were closing them at a much higher rate. If we had wanted it to at that time, our little gizmo could have become a product small companies needed. We knew the market was changing and it didn't make sense to take that product to market, but it could have gone many different ways. By consistently identifying opportunities to connect the dots for other people's needs, you're able to identify growth in a sustainable way.

It's not easy to be an agent of change for even the healthiest of organizations. The best marketers I've worked with are those who tinker, start trouble, and/or like to learn new things. They are not people who necessarily ask for permission before trying new things or follow a rigid path set by past glory. The best growth hackers I've seen are friendly but not necessarily socially outgoing. There is no one set personality type— just a general willingness to learn, measure, and persevere.

Now you'll have the mad skills to run campaigns and drive traffic with the best of them. You're going to need to make sure the site your SEOing is ready to handle the traffic, whether it be on mobile, tablet, or desktop. Optimizing your site before the campaign starts will make you more likely to succeed.

# CHAPTER 7

# Technical SEO Elements for Success

Over the years I've seen many mistakes happen in various parts of the website maintenance process. All humans make mistakes. As lovable as we are, it's simply bound to happen. We have to allow for humanity to happen and even *plan* for these errors by having a staging process. Staging servers allow us to test before we update and therefore roll out pages with minimal drama. Web development roll-outs can happen either on a scheduled date or at the developer's discretion (unscheduled). If you are clued into the *timing* of the website updates, then you can monitor for issues as well as document when changes are rolled out in analytics. If you spot a bump in traffic or a dip after an update—how handy to be able to figure out what happened! Clear annotations in analytics help everyone understand the true impact of a website's performance on SEO.

## Setting Up for Ascendency

Let the analytics for your site guide you meaningfully to understand what the user really wants from you. If visitors are staying on your site three times as long when they arrive from organic search rather than paid, consider tweaking those paid campaigns a little more or revisit where you're sending them. Site bounces from paid traffic should be analyzed separately from organic traffic, because the use cases are different.

One of the first pieces of building a website is determining the architecture. It's very popular to use tools like all-in-ones (Marketo, Eloqua, etc.) and automated help desks (Zendesk, Basecamp) because they accomplish critical tasks. Convenience often comes at a price for technical SEO. Therefore I am cautious about overuse of some tools, because each tool slows down page loads by making server requests. It is also beneficial to have control over your own content. Giving up one's own content should not be done lightly. There are instances when hosting content elsewhere is crucial for performance, like in the case of video streaming.

There was a long stretch in the mid-2000s when it was common to see third-party tools get opinionated about changing URLs completely, which users didn't necessarily trust. Then everyone got the idea to create microsites with thin content to get more links back. Eventually, penalizations started to happen so microsites fell out of fashion as an SEO tactic around 2010 and we saw the rise of subdomains. Microsites are still very much in fashion for campaigns, time-based projects, and other fun on the web. The popularity of subdomains arose via services that wanted to give a slightly more branded feel. Subdomains were once quite unpopular, because namespace configuration was difficult until widespread consolidation of hosting services like WordPress came along. There's another way to think about it: a popular strategy to add functionality to a site also generally means farming *out* content. It is extremely common in 2016 to use a subdomain within a homepage navigation for services provided, such as Zendesk for customer support or Shopify for ecommerce.

For the search engines to *recognize* the relevance of a domain, there has to be enough content there to garner user interest. Don't give all your power (content) away. The largest sites on the web either house their own content or aggregate other sites' content.

The issue with turning one's content over to another third-party content host is that with each click to an outside site, you're losing your own users. Be careful to distinguish third-party hosts from CDNs like WP Engine, and use CloudFlare so that the site gets served from servers all over the world nearest the users. Your content should remain under your own control; you can route what's coming from your server on your own domain. If you don't examine the path your own users take, you can unwittingly start kicking users out of your own site. In some cases, users are actually forced to leave the site that brought them. Ofttimes content that should really be on the homepage is housed on these outside services. There are exceptions to this, like when using a service like Medium for the company blog. One can see some benefits for using Medium as a host, because you'll be able to use a subdomain whilst getting your blog posts in front of many other eyeballs. The biggest concern with using Medium or other third-party content hosts for your blog is the potential for analytics to not line up seamlessly.

## Meta Information

Many folks still believe that SEO means simply populating your website with meta information. Meta information is a basic branding tactic, not a shortcut to success. It's a fundamental piece of search appearance. Meta titles and descriptions end up showing in search results, so for that reason alone they matter to SEO (Figure 7-1).

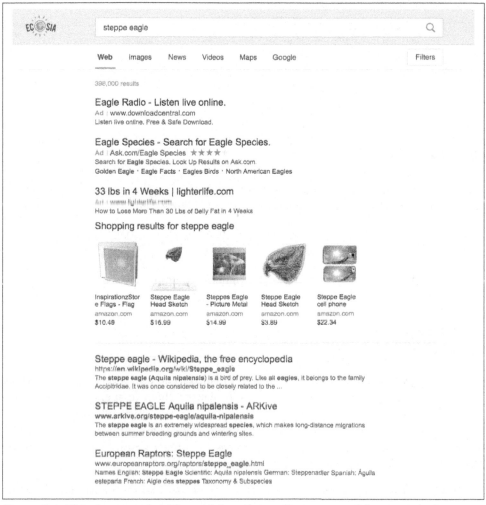

*Figure 7-1. This shows us the titles and descriptions for a query of the steppe eagle.*

In Figure 7-1 only one site *appears* to have optimized their meta description, because it's not cut off with "..." like the others. However, upon further examination of the source (Figure 7-2), it's a complete coincidence that the meta information was pulled in perfectly.

```
<title>Steppe eagle videos, photos and facts - Aquila nipalensis | ARKive</title>

    <meta name='title' content='Steppe eagle videos, photos and facts - Aquila nipalensis' />
    <meta name='description' content='Learn more about the Steppe eagle - with amazing Steppe eagle videos, photos and facts on ARKive' />
    <meta name='keywords' content='Steppe eagle,Aquila nipalensis,Birds,Animals,Chordata,Falconiformes,Accipitridae,Aves,Aquila,CITES
2,Terrestrial,Grassland,Temperate,Flying,Terrestrial,Rock,Asia,I-LC,IUCN Red List - Least
Concern,Africa,Europe,Terrestrial,Grassland,Savannah,Carnivorous,Terrestrial,Terrestrial,Mountains,Feeding,Feeding behaviour,Immature Adult,Physical
Appearance,Keoladeo Ghana NP Bharatpur,Rajasthan,India,Aigle des steppes,ARKive,endangered species,threatened species,IUCN,Red
List,images,photos,photographs,pictures,videos,films,animals,plants,biodiversity,species,wildlife,nature' />
    <meta name="DC.Title" content="Steppe eagle videos, photos and facts - Aquila nipalensis" />
    <meta name="DC.Subject" content="Learn more about the Steppe eagle - with amazing Steppe eagle videos, photos and facts on ARKive,Aigle des steppes' />
    <meta name="DC.Description" content="Learn more about the Steppe eagle - with amazing Steppe eagle videos, photos and facts on ARKive" />
    <meta name="DC.Identifier" content="http://www.arkive.org:80/steppe-eagle/aquila-nipalensis/" />
    <meta name="DC.Format" content="text/html" />
    <meta name="DC.Language" content="en-GB" />
    <meta name="DC.Publisher" content="ARKive" />
    <meta name="DC.Rights" content="http://www.arkive.org/about/terms.html" />
    <!-- End meta data -->
```

*Figure 7-2. While the site appears to have entered a meta description, it's not pulling into the search results.*

Always check the source of the site you're optimizing against what you see in the SERPs, because it's often more than meets the eye (Figure 7-3).

```
<h3 class="">Steppe eagle range</h3><div class="collapse"><p>The steppe eagle is an extremely widespread species, which makes long-distance migrations
between summer breeding grounds and wintering sites. <a href="#GlossaryTerm3" class="glossary">Subspecies</a> <i>Aquila nipalensis orientalis</i> breeds in
extreme south-east Europe, southern parts of the Russian Federation, and Central Asia as far east as eastern Kazakhstan. During the winter, it migrates to
the Middle East, the Arabian Peninsula and eastern and southern Africa. By contrast, <i>Aquila nipalensis</i> <i>nipalensis </i>breeds from the Altai
Mountains, south to Tibet, and east as far as north-east China and eastern Mongolia, and mostly winters in southern Asia <sup><a href="#ref2"
```

*Figure 7-3. After searching the text, the description that appears in search is actually the H3!*

# Site Usability

Search interest is not enough to maintain rankings; there has to also be search *excitement*. Do people come to your site and feel satisfied? The user interface is everything to SEO. Your users' experiences are critical to getting them to spend more time onsite. Designing a site with an SEO-forward approach can drastically improve a website's usability and performance. Search engine algorithms punish sites that aren't responsive to multiple form factors. Therefore, designers absolutely need to ensure their sites look flawless on every kind of device.

Usability comes in many forms, not all of them viewable to the naked eye. There's a difference between user interface (UI) and user experience (UX). User interfaces are how something appears, the look and feel. UX is the process of enhancing user satisfaction and accessibility. Usability should be the totality of any potential website visitor's experience on your URL. Try to weigh your desire to load a fun MIDI version of Louis Armstrong's "It's a Wonderful World" for all of your potential customers against the fact that they're probably on a mobile phone and will find any music disruptive. Usability is just like getting hugs; they're best when you don't think you need them.

Website development issues we are going to address include:

- UI/UX
- Staging process
- Site optimization

- Site hosting

Ensure that navigation is intuitive and make sure to include clear links in at least the footer to privacy policies, about pages, and contact pages. Quick accessibility to basic information makes a site more usable and a company appear more credible. Properly accessible information for a business will ensure the best mobile experience as well. It's also essential that your site has a clear and logical URL structure that identifies what your site is about. Logical URL formation is not the most fun thing to think about, but helps build user trust. If your company name is the coolest name ever, then use that as your URL. Too much mystery in the URL versus what is seen will make things murky for the user.

Simple and straightforward navigation generally works best. Don't get fancy with the menu options; people won't dig it. There's also no tried or true SEO benefit of a menu structure so it makes sense to go with, well, what makes sense for your respective page. Does your organization spend a fair amount of time writing amazing blogs? Great, then put blogs in your top navigation. Have you only ever gotten one press hit? Then maybe *don't* put a press page in your top navigations. I've seen companies struggle with calling press hits "buzz" instead of press because they think it's more interesting. There's no hard and fast naming scheme for the top navigation menu of your website, especially for standard pages like your company's contact pages or blogs.

When I think of logical URL structure I typically follow this schema:

*steppeeagles.com/buckets*
*steppeeagles.com/buckets/keyword-specific*

Here are some items to consider when setting up a website.

1. Testing is definitely key. There are various validators to make this easy and bulletproof.
2. If you don't provide schema data, you're leaving it up to the various platforms to make a best guess at what you want for title, thumbnail, description, etc. Providing the schema data ensures you get it right.
3. Different platforms let you choose the default sharing format for a post using schema. For example, Twitter let's you choose the layout for your shared posts. Check out the Twitter card types here: *https://dev.twitter.com/cards/types*.
4. You should check how your posts look on any platforms that you see shares coming from, even if you don't use those platforms.

Those are the main points to think about. It's as much about the social networks as it is for Google.

The first time I ever heard of a *six-pack* was when a colleague was describing the broken out results a company gets (or doesn't) under their organization's name (see Figure 7-4). If we do everything right in the URL structure of the site and the pages are weighted appropriately, we enjoy the glory that is the six-pack appearing how we want it to. Most companies I've worked with have some sort of issue with their six-pack. Don't fret—even Google does!

## Google

https://www.google.com/
Enables users to search the Web, Usenet, and images. Features include PageRank, caching and translation of results, and an option to find similar pages. The ...

### Gmail
This site won't let us show the description for this page.

### Search
Search the world's information, including webpages, images, ...

### Maps
Find local businesses, view maps and get driving directions in Google Maps.

### News
Comprehensive up-to-date news coverage, aggregated from sources ...

### Images
Google Images. The most comprehensive image search on ...

### Videos
Search millions of videos from across the web.

See results only from google.com

*Figure 7-4. Note: the Gmail description—it's hilarious! Perfection is always a noble goal.*

The consistent method I've used for getting a company's results to look the way I want it to is with clear navigation and internal linking.

Try to go easy on the JavaScript. Though it is great for making websites look pretty, be sure to use it wisely (sparingly). Too much JavaScript can have a negative impact on your performance, but typically only when it's too much.

*Clean that code.* Website creators need to keep their code nice and clean (think simplified, not bloated), which means not stuffing web pages with so much content that visitors don't have a clue what's going on. If a site has badly organized content, it confuses the users. If a site has too much code, it complicates things for search engines, which can detect problems even if the site displays properly in the browser.

Here are some ways to boost your site's performance on the server level:

1. Optimize those images by compressing them with a utility. Consider CSS image sprites and plugins like WP Smush.
2. CSS image sprites are very useful because they put less stress on the server (unless you've already pushed to HTTP/2, which allows you to have numerous simultaneous downloads without having to establish a new connection for each one). Google advises against this now as they are way into HTTP/2. Using CSS3

techniques for styling your webpages can boost performance better than leaning on JS can. This keeps it cleaner.

3. Combine HTML5 with CSS3. These two work in tandem to make sites sleeker, cleaner, and faster. HTML5 provides lots of advanced functionality compared to older HTML, and is flexible so it can be scaled down as your media requires. CSS3 not only reduces page loading times but also helps give sites a more interactive feel about them. Just be sure that your code is kept squeaky clean so the HTML validates properly.

What truly comes at the heart of usability? The user. I have spent so much time advocating for the user that it now comes as second nature. Every SEO has to consider the usability of a site as a factor that matters for success. Interactive elements are fun and, when done correctly, they enhance a user's experience on any given website. The issue with elements done in scripting languages or external programs is that they can bog down the browser mercilessly. Always try to consider that the person coming to your site won't have a single asset cached, so unless you're super deliberate about using a scratch browser to test, any new users will have a longer load time than you do. Avoid using Flash and other interactive elements that will adversely affect performance. Flash technology has largely become obsolete, so it's best avoided if you're building a new website. Many devices and browsers aren't even compatible with Flash, or they simply block it altogether.

---

### Clean Browsers

As a search practitioner, you have to accurately perceive the battleground you're on in order to attain successful outcomes. Projects fail for numerous reasons, but not always because of what's happening online. It's imperative to perform, at the very least, a cursory search on various platforms before hiring or working with anyone—even a potential client.

I also recommend searching two varieties of browsers: the one you use all the time and then some scratch browsers. The scratch (test) browsers are ideal to do extra non-cookied, not-logged-into-anything searches. I call these *clean* searches. An easy way to create a new scratch browser is to establish another guest account on your own machine and not import any bookmarks or logins to that user's browsers.

Personal note: I use scratch browsers for purchasing travel tickets as well, because prices go up fast once you start accumulating cookies.

---

# Setting the Stage

This section will cover the staging process, site hosting, and optimization. There are no formal standards, but there are definitely some best practices in terms of website performance. Mobile users *demand* speed without provocation. The amount of time a user will wait for a site to load decreases more and more over time. Projects like Facebook's Instant Articles and Google's Accelerated Mobile Pages (AMP) project are spoiling users with amazing load times. The rest of the world's hosts will have to catch up, too.

Websites designed and implemented without forethought (for the audience) do not perform as well as those that have considered them. Are you loading a bunch of junky CSS? Are your cache expirations set? Take out the trash; optimize the code. Think about how many subdomains you're using and servers you're maintaining. Don't cut corners on performance optimization; deploying a WordPress template out of the box isn't good enough anymore, at least not for mobile. There are some out there that are fast, but you may as well build your own if you can.

Just like acid-wash jeans, fun webby doodads eventually go out of style (and only come back in style "ironically"). Toss out your pop-ups and Flash on mobile sites. Keeping poorly performing older elements will no doubt alienate site visitors and send them packing. If you have to utilize ads on your websites for revenue, there are more subtle ways to do this than flyovers on mobile. There are ways to monetize that do not alienate your users.

There are logical places to cut costs in a marketing department, but they should be based on operational need. Following W3C is always advisable for validation. By following modern standards, you promote common data formats and exchange protocols, known as RDF.

Hosting is not the place to cut costs, ever. Would you cheap out on the foundation of your house? No. Bargain-basement hosting is a bad idea. Avoid the cheapest ISP hosting packages because they will try and often succeed to failboat your SEO efforts with CDN hijacking. A company *should* own search juice from its own content and go as smart as possible on hosting. There's a sweet spot. $20-$30/month is worlds better than $5/month. The super cheap hosting crams tons of sites onto the same box, making performance unpredictable and making you vulnerable to security breaches if the other sites are poorly implemented, which they probably are if they're on cheap shared hosting. Larger hosting packages allow the webmaster to customize and optimize all the right stuff. Avoid bloated API packages for tools and services, as they can slow things down dramatically. Ideally, the host would be HTTP/2-compatible so that speed and performance are as premium as possible.

Secure Sockets Layer (SSL) is the de facto security technology for creating encryption between a web server and a browser. Data that is passing between a web server and browsers must stay secure. Instances like taking payments or sharing private information on mobile will always call for enhanced security. SSL on a website is the bare minimum level of security that should be performed, whether it's mobile or desktop.

## SSL for Everyone!

"SSL everywhere" is the rallying cry of Let's Encrypt (*https://letsencrypt.org*), an emerging, free, automated, and open certificate authority (CA). It's a non-profit that endeavors to become part of the plumbing of the internet. So cool. They are even working on their own protocol named Automatic Certificate Management Environment (ACME) to de-chore-ify the entire process. I am a fan of anything that helps democratize the internet and enhances security at the same time.

In that vein, if HTTP/2 and the like are increasingly requiring SSL, we must ask why aren't all sites using it? Administering SSL certificates can also be a chore. So potential costs coupled with inconvenience cause many developers to put SSL deployment off until later (or just skip it entirely to save workload). Bad move! Security certificates are essential to the health of secure website. Self-generated certificates are not a great solution, because not only does everyone have to click through scary security screens, but it's more scary than no padlock at all. A scary experience lowers the bar of sensitivity to scary security screens thus making security adoption far worse for everyone in general.

While I cannot endorse any specific hosting services or packages, I would suggest reading user reviews along with industry expert reviews (or endorsements). If one service is slightly costlier than another but has more bells and whistles that you need, *the internet will tell you* if the potential upgrade is worth it or not. Depending on resources available, some managed services are pricey but worth it.

Try to avoid unknown or international hosting companies unless there's a compelling reason, like you are running an international site yourself. The main reason to avoid them is the support; it's hard to get tech support when your schedules are flipped. Also, sometimes standards can be different among countries and you don't want to be a victim of circumstance.

### Don't Get a House on Spam Street

Working with a large and spammy host can result in some issues you may or may not realize. You can be judged by the company you keep (on the C block). I've heard many SEOs refer to the "Bad IP Neighborhood" which means your IP could be in range of spammers. Oh noes!

There are a number of utilities you can run to find the quality of your IP neighborhood, so no need to worry.

# The Block and Tackle

From server speed to CMS systems and their by-products, there are technical elements in need of handling. This section will cover the basics of technical elements to consider with regard to SEO. When we fail to consider what's happening behind the scenes, we fall behind in terms of site performance. It's not easy to optimize a site, pull out unused CSS, and reduce bloated JavaScript, but with hard work your site can reap the rewards. Strike a balance between JavaScript code size and the functionality it's meant to serve.

It's good to think of the browser like an operating system or a compiler. Every script and piece of tracking we deploy within a site is essentially a piece of software we are making the browser sift through. Leaving junk in the source code for the user to download leads to longer load times. Until you're able to migrate to HTTP/2, it's good to stay hyper aware of what assets are looming on a site's servers. Too much hang time on load starts to feel like downtime to the user, which means they'll click away. A user that has bad experiences on your site is not likely to come back. In the worst case, a user will go to social media or networking sites and out you.

### Too Much Tracking Gets Tacky

It's rousing for marketing departments to start learning more about user behavior. We acquire bounteous user information by throwing in an egregious amount of tracking scripts. Eventually we will ask the browser to do too much. We're using the browser as software, but we're also asking the browser to compile software on-the-fly.

Cache is king. Use the cache! Many developers use out-of-the-box WordPress templates to save time and expense. It's OK to use templates, but they typically do not have performance-related bells and whistles for superior performance. If you don't have the resources, then try a host like Medium (*http://www.medium.com*), which will host you for free and give you access to a sizable content network distribution. However, Medium does not plug in any outside analytics tools yet, which is unfortunate.

# Site Architecture

Setting up a site properly and logically enhances the user experience and therefore SEO. It's crucial to think about the future of a site, not just the current day. If you think hierarchy is a golden ticket, this is not true.

Developers and marketers should work together to build the following technical strategies thoughtfully:

- Network topology

- Subdomain management
- Meta Information

There's a fair amount of confusion when it comes to subdomains and SEO. It's been debated whether subdomains (*cool.steppeeagles.com/*) are better to use than subdirectories (*steppeeagles.com/cool*).

The trick of diverting juice amongst properties on your own servers within a domain is over. There was a time when subdomains or microsites could be used to boost credibility between sites. It's more important to be consistent in your architecture than to pick one precise method.

Personally I prefer subdirectories to other alternatives like different domains because the former do not keep all content under the same roof. It's far better for your future site management to keep them in the same tent, however I cannot report in ten years any appreciable difference in performance for subdomains over subdirectories. Google has said (*https://youtu.be/9h1t5fs5VcI*) that hierarchy is up to the individual site operator and no magic can be gained by implementing either one. A compelling use case for deploying subdomains is when you're performing SEO for sites in multiple languages.

Another consideration for webmasters and SEOs alike is dynamic versus static URLs. If you choose one versus the other for URL structure, it isn't the end of the world. If your pages are completely different, dynamic service may be the only way to go. Static pages are increasingly popular for performance reasons.

## Site Canonicalization

When you change a URL, be sure to redirect it correctly. Do not trust that the user will work to find out where your content really is; they're already gone. The best change for the user to have is no change at all. So zen, right?! But seriously, pick one methodology early, and then stick with it. Document structures accordingly.

When teams grow and personnel changes happen, the details of server configurations can become hard to keep track of. Even query strings can throw off the best of the algorithms. Remember, we *want* robots to know what we're doing. This solves the duplicate content problem. We always have to consider what works from the perspective of the robot.

Canonical URLs/namespaces are an important computing concept to understand. A canonical URL is a container or holder in computing lingo that describes related objects, which makes it possible to distinguish between different items. Another way to think about the namespace is a hierarchy of files and directories. Normalize the namespace! Think about it. It's kind of fatuous how many patterns for the same thing there are in the most commonly used web servers.

For Apache/NGINX, these are the common patterns:

- *www.steppeeagles.com/article/*
- *www.steppeeagles.com/article/index.html*
- *steppeeagles.com/article/*
- *steppeeagles.com/article/index.html*

For IIS, the situation is even worse, depending on version:

- *http://www.steppeeagles.com/*
- *http://www.steppeeagles.com/default.asp*
- *http://www.steppeeagles.com/default.aspx*
- *http://steppeeagles.com/*
- *http://steppeeagles.com/default.asp*
- *http://steppeeagles.com/aspx*

It's case insensitive.

If you don't have redirects all over the place, use canonical URLs as thoughtfully as possible. Pick a style and then stick with it; consistency is the key to easy updating.

Here are a few things to consider about canonicals:

- A good canonical structure looks something like this: `<link rel="canonical" href="http://steppeeagles.com/blog" /> <base>`.
- 302 redirects are worthless. If you think about it, it actually makes sense. I mean, it's a *temporary* redirect.
- Either one's OK, but "www." being secondary is the cool trend these days
- Best bet, don't monkey with it! No sojourns. Even a 301 redirect can cause a 15% drop-off.

# Video Handling

For many years short videos have been rising in popularity, because people like to snack on media, not have a whole dinner. A short video with captions can really enhance a site's ability to present information to visitors. Mary Meeker's (*https://en.wikipedia.org/wiki/Mary_Meeker*) annual trends report always reveals a pantheon of scintillating data revelations and predictions. In 2016 (*https://youtu.be/334Gfug5OL0*) she predicted the overwhelming domination of video and video platforms as a means for content distribution. The adoption numbers are staggering and there's no denying that video is the king! We want to enjoy little bits without much thought and often we can with little to no consequence within the realm of social media.

We like to watch our videos on social and to keep them short, sweet, and captioned. Videos with captions allow the user to watch in silence while at work or anywhere else. The interesting part is while video is thriving, due to the silence, video advertising is suffering (*http://bit.ly/2lxrIbc*). Social media endorsements are at an all-time high; YouTube is actually considered one of the top search engines that everyone tries to remember to SEO. Video SEO shouldn't be an afterthought, and it's not as simple as punching in some keywords for the descriptions.

Don't forget about thumbnails! Video previews are way more important than people give them credit for. Make sure the thumbnail is a true depiction of what the user is expecting to see. Tricking a user is never a great idea.

Streaming video can be done through sites like Ustream (*http://www.ustream.tv*), YouTube (*https://www.youtube.com*), Vimeo (*https://vimeo.com*), Daily Motion (*http://www.dailymotion.com/us*), Vine, and Instagram. Video chat services are Facebook Live, YouNow (*https://www.younow.com*), Periscope, and Twitch (*http://www.twitch.tv*).

---

## YouTube SEO Tips!

Video SEO always has a twist to it because the hosting tends to be external. YouTube is one of the largest search engines, so we must think about it in terms of search.

Although the maximum description length is 5,000 characters, they trim that to 120-160 characters in the search results. The most important part is the first sentence of the description. Lead with the part you want to be read.

For any of the keywords that you've entered, it's generally good practice to include them at least once in your description. However, the description needs to feel organic, so you don't want to stuff keywords into sentences just for the sake of including them. If you can't find room for them, better to leave them out. Add a link back to a relevant blog post immediately after the first sentence. You may need to experiment to get the placement right, but when it's done correctly the link will show up above the "show more" button.

---

# CMS Management

Content management systems make for the easiest updating of websites by various technical competencies across an organization. Many companies utilize a CMS system for website management and this is expected to continue for the foreseeable future. These systems come with all sorts of plugins, tools, and predesigned templates. Without a web development background it's difficult to discern what you're getting with a package or the purchase of a website from a contractor or agency.

Setting up CMS systems on websites is fairly straightforward, but clearing out the junk that comes with these systems is far more difficult. Templates are very easy to come by in the world of popular content management sites like WordPress (*https://wordpress.org/*), Joomla (*https://www.joomla.org/*), Prismic (*https://prismic.io/*), or Ghost (*https://ghost.org/*). How to pick a theme depends on the amount of resources you have available to deploy the site, and also to maintain it. If your budget is modest, you probably want to keep it simple so you don't need a developer for text updates; this is where the CMS really starts to shine.

It's difficult to predict the future in any situation, much less a web server environment. Picking a theme on a third-party site is a delicate balance of trust. It's good to look for the frequency with which updates are made and how effectively the theme's creator is in repairing bugs. There's no perfect theme, and it's not possible to find a bug-less one. It is OK to go rogue and create your own theme if the project's web developer is experienced enough, but always remember the thing about islands, which is that they can get lonely.

If you're using a prebuilt solution with lots of stuff you may not need, then you'll want to reduce the footprint on your server; it's inevitable (Figure 7-5).

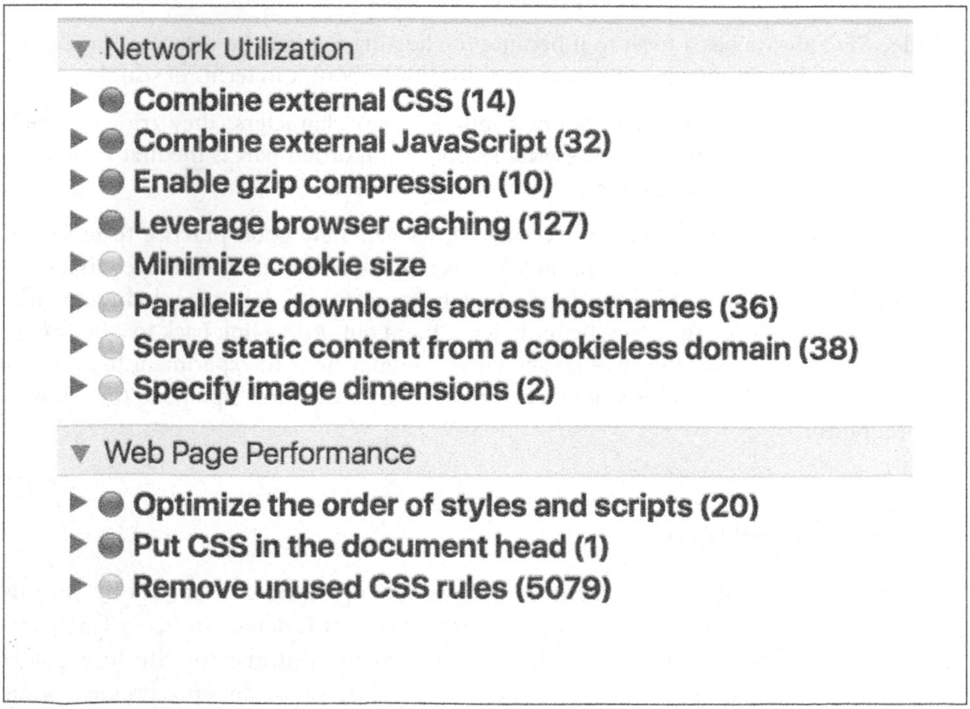

▼ Network Utilization

▶ ● **Combine external CSS (14)**
▶ ● **Combine external JavaScript (32)**
▶ ● **Enable gzip compression (10)**
▶ ● **Leverage browser caching (127)**
▶ ● **Minimize cookie size**
▶ ● **Parallelize downloads across hostnames (36)**
▶ ● **Serve static content from a cookieless domain (38)**
▶ ● **Specify image dimensions (2)**

▼ Web Page Performance

▶ ● **Optimize the order of styles and scripts (20)**
▶ ● **Put CSS in the document head (1)**
▶ ● **Remove unused CSS rules (5079)**

*Figure 7-5. This is the typical amount of resources that come with a WordPress templated site, found in Chrome Developer Tools audits.*

So you'd like to start a CMS project. What do you ask the developer for?

1. Remove unused CSS, but test all pages. Sometimes subpages use CSS that the homepage doesn't.
2. Choose a host that has deployed both HTTP/2 and IPv6. If not, it should be in the roadmap.
3. Put JavaScript in the footer when possible to increase load performance, but know that this can impact analytics capture in certain cases.

---

## Testing in a Clean Browser

So many times we've rolled out website changes and updates to have the client tell us "No, we don't see this." Technically speaking, they do not see the changes because they haven't refreshed the cache of the browser. They often simply hit the refresh button in the browser. Hitting the refresh (arrow) in conjunction with the shift key refreshes browser cache.

*Figure 7-6. Note the arrow shaped in a circle to the left of the home button*

Style sheet changes aren't always apparent, so I like to keep a "clean browser." An SEO should always keep a clean test environment, which means a browser that has no sign-ins, no cookies, and no cache.

---

While content management systems offer everyone in an organization the easiest possible method to update a website, they tend to have drawbacks in performance when left un-groomed. It's typically OK to use a CMS over expensive proprietary systems or expensive monthly support contracts. It's better to have the website be regularly updated and relevant to potential site visitors than tuned to the hilt like a sports car.

Performance and usability are no joke when it comes to search and usability. To give users a positive experience is to retain more search economy, because what's good for the user is good for search. Each visit that's made is a vote for your site, so make it count.

You're well on your way to getting into the sweet, sweet technical search zone now. We've covered a heavy amount of technical theory and best practices in this chapter. Let's talk mobile next, because it's a *slightly* different battlefield. While mobile and desktop SEO share the same practices, they diverge in ways that we'll cover in the next chapter.

# CHAPTER 8

# Mobile Search

Traditional rules that we understood as SEOs went out the door with mobile and that's OK. Bounce rates, user journey, session duration, and all other user behavior metrics should be examined carefully on mobile. The data is there and it's layered. When turning on your GPS and other features of the phone, some privacy is lost. Embrace it, but turn and *admit* the strange as we start to intrude further into people's lives.

We started to see sharp increases in mobile searches along with changes in user behavior after the launch of the iPhone in 2007. A decade later, the SEO field has firmly dropped anchor into the mobile search ocean. One of the first things to recognize with mobile search is that it's increasingly different than desktop's search results. The input methods have also changed with mobile search.

## The Lay of the Land

When mobile surpassed desktop in monthly searches in 2014, the entire search industry took notice. On April 21, 2015 Google rolled out an algorithm update that went down in history as *mobilegeddon*. Google's change in algorithms was intended to rank higher search results for sites that met mobile-friendly criteria. The belief was that the update happened because many sites weren't properly taking into account the meteoric rise of mobile.

Despite the dramatic sounding name, mobilegeddon was not the disaster people predicted it to be. What it did for SEO as an industry was to thrust mobile usability into the arena. To remain competitive, SEOs finally realized they needed to meet the demands of their new mobile target audience. It was a wake-up call.

The mobile battlefield is changing by the day, physically and metaphorically due to continuous rapid advancements in processing power coupled with machine learning.

Data previously in silos is now being connected. Between mobilegeddon and Google's Accelerated Mobile Page project (AMP), it's clear that technical performance must *constantly* improve to achieve mobile search dominance.

Overall, mobile SEO's evolution has occurred considerably faster than conventional desktop growth has. Search is now the most common starting point for product-based queries on mobile. About half of mobile searches begin with search engines, one-third begin on branded websites, and a quarter begin on branded apps.

The search game has changed *forever* in both the technical and financial senses. Mobile's popularity means users of the technology have a #winning life, because new leaders are still emerging. Just as the great Taylor Swift has predicted, we're gonna *shake it off*. A business can become a business in minutes on mobile with a storefront and a payment processor. Players like Square (*https://squareup.com/*) and other payment gateways for mobile have commutated what marketers can do.

We're no longer married to the old concepts of how we spend our money online, so the big players feel a stronger sense of humility as they haven't *put a ring on it* (us) yet.

> Even in the U.S., Google is confronted with signs of trouble. Google is no longer the #1 search engine for *product searches*. That title now goes to Amazon. And Amazon is pulling further ahead. In 2016, 55 percent (up from 44 percent in 2015) of consumers use Amazon to search for products, while only 28 percent (down from 34 percent) use Google.
>
> —Soeren Stamer (*http://bit.ly/2nw6dbo*), VentureBeat

# All SERPs Are Not the Same

Mobile search will only continue to converge from desktop until desktop starts to morph *into* mobile because it's been outmoded. More than two-thirds of organic searches display different results on desktop versus smartphone. I've already started seeing companies use the collapsed mobile hamburger menu on all platforms to simplify design. *Every* platform must be optimized with a keen eye and noble heart, because tablet varies from phablet which varies from smart watch, etc. The subtle differences will grow. We will only continue to see results diverge further between mobile and desktop; the delta is ever-widening.

One of the strongest use cases for prioritizing mobile SEO optimization is local search. Nearly half of all consumers who do a local search on their phone also visit the store within a day. Mobile search is dramatically more semantic and conversational in nature than desktop.

So how can we dive deeper into these concepts? To know where we're going, we have to look back at where we've been; even on the web, history matters.

> I have a dream for the Web [in which computers] become capable of analyzing all the data on the Web—the content, links, and transactions between people and computers. A "Semantic Web," which makes this possible, has yet to emerge, but when it does, the day-to-day mechanisms of trade, bureaucracy and our daily lives will be handled by machines talking to machines. The "intelligent agents (*https://en.wikipedia.org/wiki/Intelligent_agent*)" people have touted for ages will finally materialize.
>
> —Tim Berners-Lee

Most people think of the internet as "the web" and then think no further, but that notion is long, long gone. The web is what we see in our browsers (and search engines), but it goes so much deeper and some people don't think or care to know the difference. Another way to look at it is, before the web there was the 'net. You could download a program from across the country but it took a few hours to get there sometimes. It's the same with traditional databases: the web is the filesystem. Before the web, there were fun things like telnet and BBSes. Fidonct! After the web came other interesting bits and pieces that go in and out, from mobile SDKs and APIs to any number of extravagant fun things.

Some of my colleagues were once against preparing for mobile, citing that the top search results were dominated by paid results. It's true that advertisers have been taking advantage of geolocation tools a little longer than organic marketers since our great smartphone infatuation began nearly a decade ago. But how quickly things change around us. Organically we must master mobile on the green pasture that it is and think through how the information flows. All of the information we put out there is not hanging out on a lonely boat. There are giant graphs that grow by the minute, charting all of the information. Bing, Ecosia, and all other search engines will continue to cultivate their knowledge graphs.

You may have heard of the infamous social graph (*https://en.wikipedia.org/wiki/Social_graph*). Or maybe open graph? You can use both if you want. Facebook hasn't really talked about any open graph support, so you decide! If you add all of the data together about information flow, it's exciting. With machine learning technologies, human-readable content is being processed PLUS machine-readable data. The web means something different. Vast networks are connecting everything and so we must think more globally. We know about the web, yes, but there's so much data floating about. How does it connect, you may be thinking.

Data previously in silos is now being connected, and in some cases, mixed together. For example, IBM claims Watson has read thousands of research journals and that it can read millions of books in minutes (*http://cbsn.ws/2mDStaa*). If you couple machine learning (ML) with so much data, the possible applications are endless. With machine-learning technologies, content is being processed in addition to the machine-readable data. The data that we're sending all around us 24/7 is not necessarily human-readable.

In 2007 Tim Berners-Lee first introduced us to the semantic web (*https:// www.w3.org/standards/semanticweb*). Things swelled and life became bigger than the WWW. Web 2.0 had everyone electrified for a while, but the next wave (Web 3.0) started showing us that there was something more for us than discrete web pages. *New global applications are a matter of abstraction.* We're now moving towards the Giant Global Graph (GGG) as a way to understand the search landscape, which is essentially the *meta* version of the semantic web. It's not *technically* a successor, but industry experts say they used the previous work as inspiration. So it's more of a best-in-breed adaptation than a continuation—more of a "continuation in spirit" than anything else.

The mobile SERPs depend on the phone, browser, and location. Context is what the mobile applications truly seek to find. The additional variance is the *where and how* the search on mobile happens: if it is in a browser, another site, or an app, and whether it is done by text or voice input.

## Local Search

Mobile search results differ from other platforms in that the results are, well, more locally focused on geography and immediacy. The browser uses the phone's GPS and whatever else it can scrape together from the OS to serve up desirable options nearby. Local search is often held up as the golden chalice of mobile SEO for good reason. Consumers are increasingly using their phone to locate purchases in-store and then make the purchase close by, not necessarily online. Local merchants cornering their mobile search turf will reap great financial rewards.

Local search strategies vary depending on many factors, but there are extra basics to *always* cover no matter what. For local SEO, it's important to always *mind the "NAP"* (name, address, phone number). Despite the outward simplicity of the NAP, it is still the most common local SEO issue I see smaller businesses struggle with. Another common issue with local SEO that big and small businesses alike struggle with: reviews and social media. Review sites can run the gamut of Amazon, Yelp, Glassdoor, or reviews tied to Google Maps. Be sure to try for consistency across your listings, regardless of platform: the Yelp listing should absolutely match Google Maps listings and the company website and so on. If there's been a change or expansion in business location, act accordingly. The city and state should also be included in the title, which helps for indexing as well as trust.

*Proximity is money.* We have to ask ourselves, are directions searches? Like, maps and stuff? Yes, just ask Google or Apple. It's important to make sure information shows in a map search the way it should. Some databases actually have location-enhanced data types for this and other purposes. Consideration of a map algorithm doesn't necessarily need to become part of your search strategy. Schema is one of the most important things (if not the most) to get right for local search. When done correctly, schema can help display information automatically in mobile SERPs so users can click and get directions (Figure 8-1).

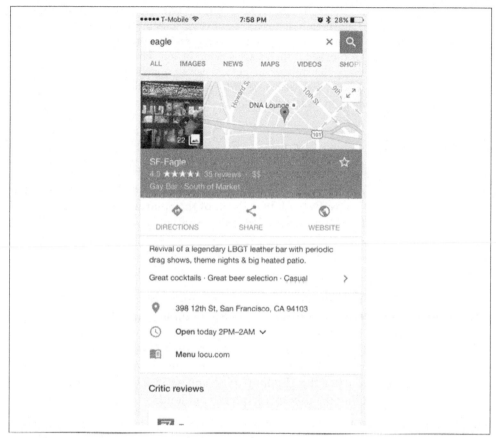

*Figure 8-1. A mobile search for "eagle" was assumed to be for directions because I was searching from an iPhone.*

Mobile, local organic search is tremendously powerful for a local business. More than half of us want to use an address or phone number we see in an advertisement, which users fully expect to be customized via city and zip code. Nearly two-thirds of smartphone users (*http://pewrsr.ch/2mczwMg*) use it to get directions or call buttons from the phone.

Local reviews can also be powerful in garnering increased local search. Many people use reviews of others to make a decision about whether or not to visit a local business. Competitive research is time well spent in any given local business market to help determine the best course of future action.

# Mobile Voice

Search inputs are changing from text only to include speech, motion, sound, and location. SEO is not ending, it's actually beginning to happen on a whole new level. Search continues to evolve with the advent of the applications and experiences: voice, lightning port devices, augmented realities, and virtual too. There are infinite realms for mobile search we are only just starting to discover. Savvy SEOs will see the "Wild Mobile West" for what it really is: a search battlefield that's constantly changing scenes.

Text-to-speech device technology is rising quickly. Using voice commands on mobile phones signals the entrance of an additional form of input where queries are conversational (i.e., "Where is the closest gas station?"). The semantic and conversational nature of voice search makes it inherently different than text-based searches. Long-tailed keywords make up 70% of searches, increasing the ability of search engines to supply relevant results. After the Hummingbird update in 2013, Google added in a microphone icon, enabling the user to ask queries out loud.

I'm not sure if its 100% true, but I've heard from many sources that the main reason most computer voices are female is because of the movie *2001: A Space Odyssey*. Allegedly, computer voices were once predominantly male, but the computer voice of HAL freaked people out so much that for the next 20 years machine voices became increasingly female.

SEOs should consider that if they're optimizing for mobile search on Google they have to plan for the direct answers box, also known as *rich answers*. The direct answers box allows the user to see a small preview of what's contained on the destination page, along with the page title and URL. We can assume that search engines will want to use direct answers for voice search results on mobile.

Potential voice search services include products like Apple's Siri, Google Now, and Microsoft's Cortana. Amazon's Alexa is voice-controlled search for the web, but also for services like Amazon.com fast ordering. Retailers will be well served to optimize their Amazon listings for voice command. There's a significant fiscal benefit in making the user's experience as frictionless as possible for quick ordering on mobile. Mobile conversion remains a bit tricky on voice, especially for advertisers. Using voice search commands on mobile means advertisers are unable to show ads, because people are not looking at the phone.

Voice command accuracy improves continuously and exponentially with processing power and machine-learning advancements. We can also assume that search engines will want to use direct answers for voice search even though they are more difficult to advertise on (*http://read.bi/2my2061*).

We know there are tons of people using mobile phones while driving or doing any number of things. Have you ever seen sheer panic in the face of someone who thinks they've lost their phone? Mobile phones are *always* close to those who use them. Even closer lurk home devices that remain omnipresent.

With the advent of the smart home, our device relationships have changed a fair amount. Digital assistants can help make things easier around the house or office. For those not utilizing Siri or Alexa, there are Google's rich answers. When we use digital assistants, our queries are natural language. SEOs can benefit by using digital assistants to understand mobile purchasing queries. I like to have fun with it.

---

## Vocal Digression

Below are a few questions I've asked various digital assistants. It's funny to see how the assistants pull up things for you via voice search. Sometimes we can search for silly things.

**Amazon Echo:**

Me: "Alexa, are you my friend?"

Alexa: "Of course," she cooed soothingly.

**Amazon Dot:**

Me: "Alexa, am I cool?"

Alexa: "You're cooler than cool. You're the coolest."

**Apple's Siri:**

Me: "Siri, do you love me?"

Siri: "Calling Dylan"; she abruptly called my contact without confirmation. Funny thing is that this is actually useful.

**Google Voice:**

Me: "OK, Google Now, find me some fun!"

---

> Google: Pops up maps listing to an actual place in San Francisco called *Find the Fun Productions (FtFP)*.
>
> Sadly, there were no reviews for FtFP. Perhaps someday!

To get to the top of a returned voice query, the format must match the style, which is typically conversational. The humdrum largesse of inquests we demand of digital assistants are often phrases like, "Call home," "What time is it?" or "Give me directions to the pizza palace." Think of your queries as a question you're asking a person who doesn't speak the same language as you—keep it concise. When we ask voice questions, the digital assistant will pull results from different areas like email, the web, social media, and even saved local files.

## Mobile Design

With over 100 billion (*http://zd.net/2mcBufY*) searches per month on mobile, there's no need to argue whether or not design matters for mobile. It does. When I want information about a company, I always look at both desktop and mobile experiences. If a site appears to be super tiny and hard to zoom, then it's nonresponsive on mobile. It's also a strong indicator that they're probably not SEO-conscious, so they'll need your help! Performance and optimization are the key elements to mobile SEO success, so let's explore what that really means.

The latest few editions of Google's mobile SEO guidelines have had a much bigger focus on website design. This makes sense because we know that websites often display far differently on mobile devices than on desktops or laptops. Sometimes there are vast differences between tablet and phone or even phablets. It's the Wild, Wild West for website creators; for usability alone you must consider a dozen platforms. If we're talking mobile apps, there's quite a bit more to consider, like linking strategies or data capture between all of the nitty-gritty layers. Responsive sites in the true sense make the most sense for many projects.

Deploying a responsive design for your website is a smart alternative to coding a separate desktop and mobile version. This type of design is recommended as one of a few basic mobile website types for a few reasons. The first is that the actual content on the page is the same no matter what device you will use to access it, with identical URLs. Responsive design also chops down many potential duplicate content problems, which can lead to penalization. The only thing that changes with responsive design is the CSS used to control the page rendering. Responsive designs will only take you so far, so make sure your phone number is clickable. Give users the easiest possible method to reach out to you. Test and test again. Scrolling is the de facto activity on mobile. Mobile users are especially unforgiving when it comes to clicking off a page or app.

Site practitioners should test a site's tap targets for various platforms and finger sizes. Sometimes touch can be more crude on the iPhone than on an Android device, for example. People have all sorts of finger shapes. What was once clickable on a website with a mouse is now replaced by the touch of a human finger. We're no longer in a world where clicking is how to *get there*.

A few things to keep in mind for mobile usability in your design:

- It's easier to reach the bottom of the screen with our thumb than the top of the screen.
- It may make more sense to put *key* buttons at the bottom of the screen if they need to be clicked often.
- Think about what reasonable spacing with header images and menus looks like on mobile.
- Find designs that function equally for large and small fingers alike.

Forms should require fewer fields on mobile. The additional fields can be requested later, but you shouldn't make users fill out too much on their phone. That's just inconsiderate.

## Life with an Nth Screen

Many companies struggle with deciding which platforms to optimize for or build upon. We're talking about smartphones, tablets, phablets, TVs, watches, and the like. In Silicon Valley, many companies view the iPhone as the one and only platform, always and forever. It is actually kind of impractical to optimize for only *one* platform or device.

If you're focusing on one platform for the sake of another, the statistics will never look as good for the neglected platform. Catch-22's have a way of becoming self-perpetuating. There's no reason to focus on *any specific platform*. Focus on the *Nth* screen (i.e., the merging of all devices, people, and surroundings) to create a shared digital environment. In the mobile advertising world, the Nth is already *a thing*, but it hasn't quite made it over to SEO yet.

The Nth screen is the omnipresent screen we marketers all want to be on. How many screens are there in your home? I introduced this concept after having my pupils dilated as part of an eye exam. On my way home, I felt panic because I could not read a single screen. The proliferation of unreadable screens surrounding me for my short commute made me finally realize how many screens there actually were, from bus stops to grocery stores. All I saw was blur. I became hyper aware of the amount of screens we live with. As SEOs, it is our new job to get ourselves onto those screens (Figure 8-2).

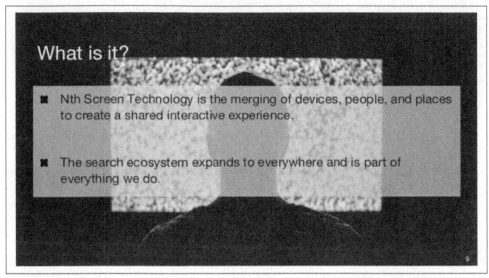

*Figure 8-2. A slide (http://bit.ly/2mxUzM0) from my Mobile SEO presentation at the SEJ Summit in Santa Monica, CA in May 2016.*

We web marketers have long obsessed and toiled over the fold. What is visible on the page without action is what gets us to scroll. The foxiness of what we see before us is what makes us expend the effort to scroll. We often think the fold is new, but conceptually it's far older than we all realize. Garnering enough attention to get the turn of a page is not a new thing. Turning pages has always required effort for us humans.

Most people actually start scrolling before everything loads. This makes speed and performance of mobile pages all the more important. The most viewed area of the page tends to be just above the fold at about 550 pixels, with just 80% viewership.

Ancient book binders had to come up with enticing headlines and imagery to get people to buy. Scrolls started turning into books when the papyrus began getting folded over. We started making books and stopped making scrolls in the first century BC when Buddhist monks took the idea for bookbinding (*https://en.wikipedia.org/wiki/Bookbinding*) from India to China. What's funny is that with mobile we're actually reverting back to the world of scrolls, which were super cool thousands of years ago. Old ways become new again with SEO on mobile (Figure 8-3).

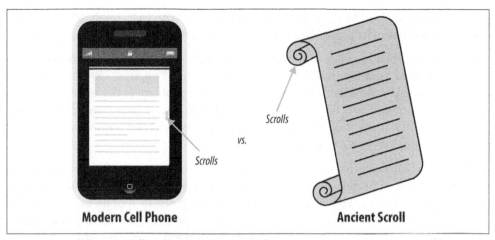

*Figure 8-3. Ancient scroll sitting next to a cell phone*

---

## Beyond the Scroll

We're growing past the concept of *the fold* as we once knew it, and people can scroll whenever they want. But what's *after* the scroll? *Is that it*? It definitely won't be the end of the UI as we know it. Zero chance. We now have this fun thing called infinite scroll and parallax scroll. *Infinite scroll* means that a page's content essentially goes forever, but it actually ends. Many webmasters deploy AJAX or Javascript to get the job done. *Parallax* hails mostly from the gaming industry and uses depth of field effects to create different effects, like the background moving faster than the foreground.

Just like the fold was an invention of necessity, the scroll had limitations built *into* the medium. What was there before the scroll? There was voice. Those with incredible recall and oration skills had the upper hand. Now we can ascend to our roles as robot taskmasters. Automation can do much of our bidding, and this trend is only going to escalate.

So, are we done yet? No, we're not! What was there before voice? There was *thought*. Research has already been done and technology developed for some auto-mind-reading technology.

---

Philip K. Dick (*https://en.wikipedia.org/wiki/Philip_K._Dick*) scenarios aside, voice input sparks innovation that could become a boon to humanity. Don't worry. Your psychic search assistant will probably get here before you know it.

Mobile content trends are moving toward longer form content than they have in the past. High-quality, longer-form, well-formatted posts with strong images and video snippets tend to outperform the shorter quick-hit posts. Text formatting is crucial so that people know how to get to the sections they want with ease; use bolded headings and big headlines to help gain mindshare in a cut-throat mobile world.

Speed is king when it comes to mobile search. Ditch your tracking that slows downloads. Kill all of your beloved email signup flyovers and popups. Do not do that to your mobile users! Another large-scale performance problem is the use of dedicated apps within a mobile site. For example, if you have videos on your page, don't require users to download anything to watch the videos. This behavior annoys mobile users and results in fewer views and video plays.

Sympathy is what you have; empathy is what you feel. At many mobile marketing conferences big and small, I've heard the lecturer tell the audience they simply need to "focus on the user." This is very common advice given to mobile developers and marketers. What does it actually mean to say "focus on the users"? Just think of your most annoying friend in high school who always whined about everything. Empathy for the user is an easy thing to say, but it's not an easy thing *to do*.

True empathy for mobile traffic acquisition means getting to know your users by studying analytics to gain insights into their behavior. Visit the site for yourself. Invite others to test it out and give feedback. When testing mobile websites, try clicking on *all of the top-level pages*, not just the home page. The majority of mobile users drop off from the site when there's bad navigation on the homepage. People are trained to expect to see the hamburger menu at this point (Figure 8-4).

*Figure 8-4. Three lines are used to denote navigation menus on mobile responsive websites. The nickname came from developers who said it reminded them of a hamburger.*

I have seen people uninstall the Facebook messenger app within seconds of installation because of chat bubbles (Figure 8-5). Other people love the bubbles and find them easy to navigate. The user's activity is always going to vary by platform, personal preferences, and prior experiences. So how do we account for that? We measure. We roll out changes in a uniform manner to the mobile site and we document those changes in analytics.

*Figure 8-5. The obtrusive chat bubble! All up in your face. Facebook would like to make their bubbles in messenger become the new style for usability. Talk about a push(y) message! Thanks to Android Central (https://www.androidcentral.com) for the image.*

It's not always easy to discern bad usability experiences for users from straight-up development problems. Some errors are purely *visual* on mobile phones. When an error is visual, that means code-checking tools cannot auto-detect them; only humans can (for now). Visual errors could be something simple like when a blog's feature image on the page renders on tablets incorrectly because it starts cutting off part of someone's face or displays text over it instead of beside it.

More complicated visual issues could be failures to resize properly, wonky navigation menus, or broken inline elements that make text appear incorrectly so that it's hard to read.

### How to Be Cool to Your Users

Testing can be automated, but there has to be a human usability element. Emulators can only go so far with simulations of usability. Mobile-friendly errors in tool consoles should always be given extra consideration.

Always adjust click targets to allow for the touch of a human finger on mobile. Tiny menus might look cute, but if they're hard to touch that's certainly not very cool to the user.

## Optimization and Performance

One of the most important facets of mobile search is performance. The infamous Google *mobilegeddon* update of 2015 heavily penalized many of those who weren't properly prepared for mobile. We're well past the age of being cool with slow performance; nobody is cool with it. Not even close.

The popularity of mobile in design became apparent in 2015 when I noticed a fair amount of desktop views of pages showing the hamburger menu. What's good for mobile performance is going to boost overall site performance at this point. When it comes to mobile performance, pages are judged individually—not the site as a whole. If your resources are insufficient for mobile optimization of the entire site, then start with the top-level pages (pages in the top navigation) and then work downwards.

---

### To Build a Mobile App or Not to Build a Mobile App?

This is a question many organizations are asking themselves right now. When done right, apps become prolific in promoting future apps. It's possible to monetize quickly if you have the right resources to deploy an app.

The trend is headed downwards for new apps. Most people get what they need and then stop downloading new ones. On average, people download 1.5 apps per month (*http://bit.ly/2mXO8kE*), depending on age group.

---

**Help Machines Help You**

- Spend the time and resources on optimization.
- Site structure and navigation matters

### HTTP/2

A lot of labor is involved in optimizing for speed on the old HTTP protocol. The original web was not designed for what we're asking it to do today. The new HTTP/2 protocol is the updated version, which allows for multiple requests. Scripts must be ordered correctly, CSS combined, and images minified. Moving over to the HTTP/2 protocol gives a speed benefit that is highly noticeable, to say the least.

As of July 2016, Googlebot does not yet crawl HTTP/2, which has kept some webmasters from wanting to make the move. At some point HTTP/2 will be a given, but until then, the enhanced speed and performance of migrating to the protocol is worth it for the improved usability and load times.

# Rich Snippets and Schema

In 2011 the major search engines came together and created a standard for markup called Schema.org. Markup has allowed webmasters to use XML to markup content by types in order to separate them. It is believed that the abuse of meta attributes and information brought this type of markup into being.

We've noticed at our agency that it's *all about the rich snippets* for mobile search performance. Schema is recognized (and in fact the vocabulary is maintained) by Google, Bing, Yahoo!, and Yandex. DuckDuckGo uses it, too.

Rich snippets are a major tool for mobile visibility and click-throughs. To start, the webmaster needs to add structured data of the right type to the site. There are generators and other tools (like the aforementioned Schema.org) that allow you to markup and then test your schema. I won't describe all of the types, but one—product snippets—is very popular in search for retailers, for example.

The author field is now *required* for snippets. Image information has gotta be locked down tight; it's very specific compared to the way things once were. Basically you should expect your image information to be 100% complete in the markup. Although schema is quite technical to deploy in some cases, there are now WordPress plugins to allow nondevelopers to join in on the fun. I have also noticed that the syntax is a bit obscure for some web developers, especially those on the junior side.

Some other types of snippets that seem to be popular are review, recipe, video, and news article snippets.

### Snippets Success Strategy

A word of caution about spending the time and resources on snippets: using them doesn't guarantee 100% that they will be displayed, especially right away. The technical nitty-gritty matters greatly in the execution of the snippet.

Also, headlines have shrunk to 110 characters down from the luxurious 166 with Google's project AMP. And the requirements are getting more and more hardcore in terms of technical performance.

Test your snippets before deploying because super wonky things can happen if you miss something as simple as entering the author field.

## Structured data versus unstructured data

Underneath the hood of every website, we have these lovely pieces of structured data. Actually, it's technically called "Schema.org structured data" if you really want to say it with the maximum amount of syllables. *Structured data* (sometimes called markup) can help more sophisticated data appear in varying results. It is a lot easier for machine-learning algorithms to chew through. Collaboration between Google, Bing, Yandex, and Yahoo is happening. Google also built their own tool (*https://www.google.com/webmasters/markup-helper*) for structured data.

The following is an example of a structured data markup:

```
<head>
<link rel="profile" href="http://microformats.org/profile/hcard">
</head>

<body>

<div class="vcard">
    <div class="fn org">SteppeEagles</div>
    <div class="adr">
        <div class="street-address">21 Searchstreet</div>
        <div> <span class="locality">San Francisco</span>,
        <abbr class="region" title="California">CA</abbr>
        <span class="postal-code">94107</span></div>
        <div class="country-name">USA</div>
    </div>
    <div>Phone: <span class="tel">+1-415-555-5555</span></div>
    <div>Email: <span class="email">nospamplz@anycontext.com</span></div>
    <div class="tel">
        <span class="type">Fax</span>:
        <span class="value">+1-111-123-4567</span>
    </div>
</div>
. . .

</body>
```

The hilarious part is the fax number.

## Project AMP

Project AMP is Google's plan to introduce accelerated mobile pages to the open web. In February 2016 Google started highlighting results (*http://tcrn.ch/2muFESp*) from project AMP in search results. All pages being equal, AMP pages have been given preferential results in Google for the first six months. It should be noted that tablets are not seen as mobile by Googlebot.

A few of my agency's clients were invited to join AMP early (several did). At first it was one of the most exciting things for mobile in a long time. The project allowed us to build web pages for static content that render crazy fast. There are three major components: AMP HTML, AMP JS, and Google AMP Cache. I am most excited about AMP Cache because it is a proxy-based content delivery network that fetches the HTML pages and caches them, which *automatically* bumps page performance.

These are the practice areas covered by AMP:

- HTML 5 (AMP HTML)
- JavaScript
- Custom styling (CSS 3)
- Global Proxy Cache

Deploying AMP can create two versions of the page, which doesn't necessarily make reporting as fun as it could be. The benefits greatly outweigh the downsides of having two separate URLs in reports. AMP pages enjoy priority in news rankings (Figure 8-6).

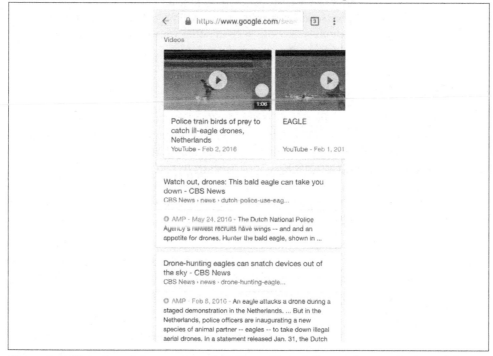

*Figure 8-6. Note the subtle mention of AMP, positioned above other results in mobile search.*

Some people are not excited about Google's new project, and AMP has started to catch some heat within the developer community. There are a subset of folks who believe AMP is nothing more than a way for Google to lock you into their ecosystem. I do agree that the company could have penalized slower sites without creating a new "standard" wherein content *conveniently* ends up on their real estate. It's certainly possible that AMP is some sort of a racket, however that's a cynical lens with which to view the world. When you get down to it, you aren't locked into much more than some *differences* in data capture (in Google Analytics) and, of course, hosting. You are always free to go elsewhere later on.

 **AMP Bounce Rates**

When first deploying AMP, don't be discouraged if your bounce rates are a little icky at first, especially when compared to desktop. You'll want to collect at least one month of data before drawing any major conclusions.

To keep improving, look at the AMP pages in analytics that received the most traffic, and compare them to the non-AMP counterpart URL. Check to see if session duration for the AMP page is higher or lower than the non-AMP page. Don't be discouraged if the numbers are off; keep iterating your visual and content enhancements! Soon you'll reap the rewards.

# Facebook Instant Articles

Forty-seven percent (*https://blog.kissmetrics.com/loading-time*) of consumers expect a web page to load in two seconds or less. Big publishers like Facebook have reaped the benefits of superior load-time performance, which they initially unleashed to a select few advertisers. On April 12, 2016 Facebook Instant Articles was released for all publishers; it was intended (*http://bit.ly/2mDEjGl*) to bring superior performance to news articles posted on Facebook. The articles are an excellent way to serve up your content faster than you can blink with a minimum of resources.

Running syndicated content is a classic SEO tactic that marketers tend to embark upon. There's a good reason for this, which is to get links back to the site (i.e., visitors and link juice). Imagine somewhere you could just post links to without much discussion, if any at all. The dream, right? Couple Facebook's infrastructure with their reach and links, and that blog could become unstoppable.

Mobile performance continues to improve dramatically, virtually month over month with the advent of projects like AMP and Instant Articles. Users will get more and more spoiled by the increase in performance for top site publishers. Once users get used to instant gratification, pages performing poorly will start to fall in the rankings. Unhappy users, especially those who are unhappy because of technical performance, will click away every time.

Technical performance is the advanced SEO's chance to shine. Though search advancement encompasses a litany of areas, technical performance is a crucial (required) element to winning the mobile battle. Let's venture on to what I like to call the fun zone, otherwise known as *case studies*.

# CHAPTER 9

# Case Studies

We'll be looking into some real-life examples of projects I've worked on, some solo and others with my team. Some were a sweet stroll to growth and others were downright abysmal. I hope that by sharing some of my experiences as an SEO at the helm, it will help you to recognize potential issues so as to avoid them in the future, whether client-side or agency.

Real names will not be used and some details have been changed to protect the innocent. Many of these cases happened while leading my own agency with clients in San Francisco and New York. I was the primary SEO for all of the accounts.

Each case study ends with what I like to call *lessons learned*.

## Multimedia Entertainment Site

The first case study is a tale of a multimedia website that offered videos featuring up-and-coming artists from many disciplines. There was little to no text at all, which presented some unique challenges. Revenue for the entertainment site came from ad monetization. SEO was their ultimate desire, because it represented an especially lucrative flow of cash for the company; to them, it was a pure gravy train with biscuit wheels. Also, ad traffic is fairly hard to resell (or upsell) because there's often a lag in data collection.

When we took over the website's management, the first step was to set up analytics instrumentation properly, then monitor traffic coming in and out. The website generated revenue for artists and advertisers mainly by the sheer amount of traffic the site got. The team who built it came from Hollywood and they had just the "right" network to get buzz. However, advertisers on the website complained that they were getting little to no value from the traffic "visiting" their ads. They were experiencing "record-low conversions," as in close-to-zero conversions. Even on a bad day, there should be a few conversions to a site that brings traffic—1% at a minimum.

Typically, sites that resell their traffic want to do so with organic, because the ad revenue is pure gravy in that scenario. You don't have to pay for organic traffic long term if you can maintain rankings, so you're essentially reselling your real estate. I liken it to owning a home and collecting rent from tenants. Also, traffic that originates from organic will tend to stay on the site for a much longer time. The upshot is that this kind of increased engagement is almost impossible to buy.

The culprit in this particular case was that the site's owners were purchasing ultra cheap paid traffic in order to resell it at a higher rate. Upon further examination, I was able to quickly determine that all of the traffic coming to the site was being sent from subdomains. I tried to visit those URLs, but they weren't anywhere close to real. Most web referral traffic comes from sites like reddit.com or t.co. The URLs can vary, but it's somewhat rare to see a subdomain providing traffic from the outset unless it's part of a campaign.

The questionable traffic was not only originating from untrustworthy URLs, the average "user" only spent three seconds or less "using" the site. Even with mobile traffic, there's just no way that any human will click off of a site within one second, much less thousands of them in a short amount of time. This didn't feel like a very likely usage pattern. So often with technology, the issues boil down to the same adage: Garbage In, Garbage Out. It became very clear to us that someone in the chain of custody was purchasing shady bot traffic (unknowingly, we hoped) and then reselling the traffic to advertisers. Sometimes the stories didn't quite add up when we asked about the details of the traffic purchases.

### A Warning About Bounce Rates

Session duration is a deceiving statistic in the case of a bounce. The user could have spent 30 seconds or 30 minutes on the page, there's no way to know definitively.

Analytics suites like Google Analytics can only measure session duration up until the last event that it captures. If a user lands on a web page, and *then* clicks the back button, the tool has no way to know how long the user was on the page. This can lead to unusually small session duration statistics when, in reality, the problem is in the capture of the data. One way to mitigate this is to record additional events such as how far a user has scrolled. By recording events beyond just page views, Google Analytics can have a more accurate basis for its measurement of session duration.

Let's just say that all the emails flying around with explanations of the fake traffic were equally as confounding. We were never 100% sure at what level the deception occurred (i.e., if the client *knew* the traffic was not coming from legitimate sources). If you're using a broker to buy third-party ads, it is best to make sure they operate above board.

**Lesson Learned:** If traffic coming from a website looks as though it is not real, then simply visit the site's listed URL. If you are receiving traffic from a website that doesn't exist in a browser, it could be a redirect or something else nonlegitimate. There are many companies trying to broker traffic deals. In many cases, the traffic is not human; it's essentially scripts or bot hackers that are run to inflate numbers, and therefore brings zero value to the site. In fact, too many bots can be a sign of trouble for an organization's overall health.

# Low Confidence, High Traffic

This next case study is for a (once) celebrated enterprise middleware services company. Their revenue model was to offer a free limited trial period. They captured users and converted them to monthly subscriptions thereafter, which were tiered. I was brought in but quickly informed that life was good because leads were "rolling in hot." There were some *kinda-sorta-maybe* looming concerns. First of all, the organization was unaware of what sort of ROI they were getting for their marketing dollars.

All kinds of information about their referral traffic was flat-out missing. The information pipeline was not merely inefficient; it was actually unknown in some areas. Therefore, they were crippled in both decision-making and planning. Because their data was too murky, they found it difficult to trust their own conclusions. Rather than looking through a murky glass, they needed some transparency. After all, data-driven decisions are what every modern organization strives for.

When the project began, cookies were fender-bending everywhere. Some of the Google Analytics UA property numbers were actually repeated three to five times in the same page. Why? Even the structure of the site became unbelievably complicated with the way that password walls were put up on the site. Complications became even more baroque when examining the setup of account and password creation. It was hard to understand where the gates were because there was no logic to it. You'd click on random things and be asked to sign in, sometimes to different systems! It was unlike any mess I'd ever seen in terms of data and general user experience.

There were over 100 full access administrators in the master analytics account. Many of the accounts (again, listed as admins) turned out to be duplicates. There were duplicates because people wanted their personal Gmail addresses in there, too. We matched over 25 names of people having both their work and personal mail as admins. They were unwilling to open another browser with their "work email" to view Google Analytics at home. This type of cavalier attitude towards building process and security led to sloppy and chaotic data collection.

When I asked seemingly simple questions in initial meetings, there were many excuses, but mostly visible annoyance, some furrowed brows, and lots of confusion. Attitudes eventually became so casual in the marketing department that almost nobody knew where traffic, users, or revenue were coming from.

In the first meeting, it became clear that we were 100% on our own to construct the picture of how this Franken-site came to be and how to fix the data leaks. Physically viewing the source of a website is generally where you want to start when looking to validate data capture. Thoroughly examine and read the site source like a novel for all top-level web pages and do not ignore the outliers.

An outlier in this case would mean custom scripts and hacks to the tracking scripts. If a routine header JavaScript filename is customized with some cutesy name, for example, you can assume someone meant for it to be there (i.e., customization has happened). Customization is a killer in a web development organization, because it facilitates mistakes and creates support dependencies. Another more subtle and hard-to-catch issue could be that, as the SEO, you run a speed test and find that something seems to hang on load. Upon further examination, you see JavaScript files with custom-feeling names. Uh-oh, time to investigate.

Every department was able to deploy nearly anything they wanted for their individual product lines. Multiple teams of web developers were updating the site without one central repository, which was the biggest reason for the physical audit of source code. Nobody seemed to notice how each new product's destination page felt like it was a new site. To click through each top-level page was a usability nightmare from the late 1990s; the headers didn't match up and sometimes the colors changed. Every page hopped to a different URL path, and some URLs jumped to subdomains. What I mean is that each new product or feature got a subdomain; sometimes an independent CMS was stitched up to it, sometimes not. When you engage with too many subdomains and CDNs, there'll be a headache. When teams of developers build individually customized sites like some kind of Winchester Mystery House (*http://bit.ly/2mDMeTP*), you are sure to have epic junk in the trunk.

Too many handshakes were happening all around. An NGINX was hooking up to one side of the site, whereas Elastic Load Balances (ELBs) were hitched to the other. The server hand-offs were seemingly random and therefore the data was too. Let's just say it was an anarchist's data rodeo given the countless servers and services involved. Once I recognized the massive overlapping in tracking scripts on individual pages, we were able to account for the discrepancies and begin to map it accordingly.

I created a spreadsheet with each top-level page URL on the site and its subpages (because they were all different). Slowly we were mapping which UA property numbers were being used and in which version of the tracking script. Very few properties were using universal analytics or tags at that point in time, so developers really liked to add their own tweaks to the scripts. Some of those tweaks included fun things like taking the tracking script and placing it in an external file used in random places or adding multiple UA numbers to the same script.

Cookie collisions are real! Sometimes the desire is there for developers to tweak. Unfortunately, the number of leads showing up as newly created accounts in GA reported more than double what was actually happening. Since nobody was actually following up on the leads, the fact that the machine broke didn't even really matter to anyone.

We helped them get ready for the acquisition by scrapping nearly all of the separate properties and bringing the data rodeo to an end. Too much complication with sub-domains meant more upkeep for them. There's nothing wrong with using subdomains, but there should be a solid reason to use them (other than a desire to not engage in communication person-to-person).

On a macro level, the ELBs were improperly configured. They had so many hand-shakes for different country sites that issues became difficult to replicate. Outages were close to impossible to fix because nobody knew where to start. A rat's nest of server topology was holding the organization back until we were able to migrate to a more stable configuration.

Everything ended up working out well for the acquisition, and data was finally able to stand up to scrutiny. With the ability to track marketing activity properly via campaigns in analytics, the company could properly determine what marketing activities brought revenue.

**Lesson learned:** Too many handshakes lead to headaches. Just because you can customize a tracking script doesn't mean you should. Document and communicate about major site changes. Do not go nuts on deploying subdomains. Complexity always grows faster than you anticipate. Avoid it if you can. Eventually, if you rely on other tools too much, you're just giving away your content while confusing users. Over-customization rarely scales well in a web development environment. Follow leading metrics, not trailing ones.

# Toxicity in Search City

Some industries are so big that the top 5% is cutthroat warfare because millions are at stake. I've only seen a handful of industries where the competing companies routinely hit the CPC maximum of $1,000 per click. If a company is operating at the level where a qualified visit can cost roughly $1,500 or more, it's safe to say that anything can happen.

When competing for highly coveted SEO terms, it's important to diversify and also focus on organic search. The company in question in this case study did not hesitate to deploy numerous SEO experts to try to dominate organic rankings. Turns out the competition did, too.

Once we were engaged as their *research* SEO firm, we quickly noticed that many new industry sites were popping up instantaneously. What we found even more interesting was that the new sites were linking to our client. As if by magic, overnight, we were the most popular girl at the prom. Unfortunately, the sites were overwhelmingly spammy in nature, as many contained the same duplicate content and weird spelling errors. We did not luck out. Someone was sinking our boat! Too many shady traffic referrers can sink a website's rankings when left unchecked.

We used the whois (*http://whois.domaintools.com*) search from domain tools to determine the main locations and hosts used by the spammy pages. The hosts were overseas and many of the registrar listings were anonymized. The nonanonymized registrar listings were to a dummy company with no phone number or physical address anywhere online. It was tempting to go and find a "hacker" of some type, but unfortunately that's not how the real world works. Even if we could have done some *TV-like hacker magic* and discovered information about the offending company, we would have put the client at risk by breaking the rules. Finding these people was a dead end for us, best pursued by the legal team.

As soon as we spotted the spam coming (obfuscation), the keyword rankings started to slip. Oh noes! Given the algorithm changes enacted earlier that year, we were correct that the client's volume of traffic would degrade quickly once these sites started to multiply. Each day, more sites materialized frenetically, all containing duplicate content along with other spammy text and links.

Fortunately, we discovered the issue before any real damage had been done. We were able to disavow the toxic links quickly and thoroughly using Google Webmaster Tools. It took several rounds of submitting the disavowals (*https://www.google.com/webmasters/tools/disavow-links-main*), a strongly worded letter to the competitor, and another nicely worded letter to the search engines to wipe the links away, but eventually the databases were updated. When all was said and done, it took a few months.

**Lesson Learned:** Do not forget to look at sites who are linking to you. When stakes are high enough and competition is steep, anything can happen—even warfare on your organic rankings. You'd be surprised by the lows that normally ethical companies will sink to when prosperity hangs in the balance. Take the high road.

# Special Snowflakes

Once we worked with a client that had the opportunity to create a new name for their flagship product after an acquisition. The only stipulation they had was that they had to change their company name completely. They were allowed to use virtually any name they wanted. This meant we were working with a new website that stood alone.

We needed this page to be able to stand and make sense on it's own, but also appear as part of a corporation (with their other brands). There were almost too many directives for us to parse, and lots of confusion at the top. So we were told by the company that the site simultaneously needed to stand apart, but be recognized as part of a bigger brand. An attitude of entitlement doesn't achieve winning results; it drains resources. This project was an interesting case of woeful ignorance, with many folks on the marketing team out of touch. Ambition is generally a positive force for a program, but not when the champagne wishes exceed SEO dreams.

The client chose a single word for their new name, which was also being used by three other companies. When we were discussing domain names, I warned that the SERPs themselves were confused about what to serve up for this particular branded query. The SERPs showed all three of the aforementioned companies first. The name was also a common word used in normal day-to-day speech.

As an SEO, it's hard to take on a project like this one because winning the war is not likely to happen. We warned continuously that to own branded search on page one would be a multiyear long-term project.

Despite my best effort to be realistic, the company still felt that they should rank on page one the same day the new site launched. We tried on multiple occasions to set expectations properly, but they felt they should just "own it." As a temporary means to reinforce the brand efforts, we used pay-per-click (PPC) for a short time. Even with a highly locked-down keyword restriction, the budget was expended in an hour or less. The quality score on the ad was fairly low since most of the people using that term had different aims. We saw painfully low conversions on branded search.

The PPC budget was a little more than $20,000 per month, which wasn't making a dent nationally at that time. So we pivoted. The short-term strategy we devised included leveraging paid social and old-fashioned elbow grease to get them traffic with social bookmarking, YouTube, Reddit, email, etc. Another thing we had working in our favor was that the client had a funny bone and let us take their social media out for a walk. Eventually the social links for Facebook pages and YouTube numbers started to look like what we wanted them to. We pulled out all the stops and grew a serious fanbase on social media, which was important for their industry. The company finally owned their name!

**Lesson Learned:** Sometimes the best battle strategy is to not to fight on the battlefield you're told to. There are rare cases when it does not make fiscal sense to build an SEO program for a business. Getting traffic funneled through social media should be considered a win, but goals don't always make sense. You have the power to change and level the search battlefield. It is more than OK to leverage paid tools like ad retargeting if they make more sense for a project.

# Too Cool for School

This project was for a privately run site that offered online training for fun and profit. Their curriculum provided students with professional hours toward certifications in many different disciplines. Somehow along the way they'd created some extremely vocal detractors online. They came to us when they had another SEO firm still engaged, because they didn't trust their firm yet. There was something about the kick-off that didn't seem quite right. They immediately sent us all the working documents that the other firm had created. This didn't feel like a good thing to us—we didn't really want or need to see a competitor's work product. But alas, unraveling the mystery began.

The content was highly technical; the SEO program was too, run 100% by spreadsheet. A previous agency created a mobile app that had very few features and yet still didn't work very well. Pride prevented them from end-of-lifing their failed native app, but that's not what became the problem. Someone who was once closely related to the company (at the top) had serious drama.

The issues we faced in our search battle were mostly bad reviews and a hint of social rage. We were assured that the company had released this person from their employ. Our research online gave us no reason to doubt the client's story that they'd simply hired the wrong person. What we had in front of us was not a salacious or sexy scandal, and uncovering the trail of information was easy. After some research we uncovered umpteen people across the country who were burned badly by this person, who we'll call Trolly McTrollTroll.

One person in particular just couldn't let it go—they wanted to burn the internet down. I would call them the epicenter troll living under our reputational bridge. Page one for a branded search of this client's name returned massively bad reviews, an active Twitter account with a similar name, a Quora post, and some blogs. Some members of the executive team took the online commentary personally. One of them decided to respond in hopes of helping the school, but it had the opposite effect.

The client had a surprisingly small and inactive social presence for an online school so we worked to build the social accounts up quickly. Building up the accounts meant simple stuff at first like filling out fields, posting interesting updates, liking other people, etc. We registered for listings on sites they didn't think of before, like individual professional associations for the subject areas. Flooding out the bad with good is often the best strategy when negative information you're trying to suppress is actually incorrect or unfounded.

Instead of continuing down the same old PPC branded campaign road, we heavily researched the organic queries. Many reputational queries were creeping in and they had low click-through rates. We added new terms to the PPC campaigns that addressed potential students who sought to understand more about the school's reputation. Next, for a customized landing page, we crafted text with targeted copy to build up reputation: quotes from graduates, press mentions with logos, and some text in the warmest font we could find to reinforce the school's position. Warm and smooth fonts to use on landing pages are Georgia, Minion Pro, or Garamond.

The school maintained an extensive list of alumni email addresses, so we ran campaigns. Some of the campaigns started out as simple surveys to gauge sentiment. Once the list was segmented out properly, we asked the students who seemed to be net promoters (*https://www.netpromoter.com*) to write a review if they had a positive experience.

In terms of reputation management we were reporting all Tweets and handles that violated Twitter's policies, including those we believed to be impersonations or bots. On Facebook, we banned people violating profanity rules or those who we believed to be our troll or subsidiary trolls. Spam reports were filed with various hosts where we could see duplicate or hate-filled comments posted. Bad reviews and commentary will vary by site, but once you've read enough fake reviews, you start to see patterns.

When we started to take the above factors into account, we knew it was likely the same person or group of people was leaving the bad reviews. We were asked to deploy "whatever methods were necessary" to search out the online detractor's true identity. After one millisecond of consideration, I declined. We instead suggested they consult an attorney, because at that point it was out of our hands. We eventually turned some of the sentiment around and attention drifted away from the controversy.

**Lesson Learned:** Always expend the effort to fully understand the goals of a search program up front and trust your instincts if something seems awry. Acknowledgement of or communication of any variety with a troll validates them (in their mind). Responding to a hateful tweet is tantalizing in the moment but only serves to make situations worse. Focus on building out better content, tuning social, and leveraging attention for positive things that are happening. Heck, knock yourself out and throw a press release out there too—it can sometimes trick news results.

# Classic Growth Hackin'

This project was one of those during which we kept high-fiving constantly because the money was rolling in steadily. When the chemistry is right for both agency and client, magical things can happen. Strong communication between marketing and product development will only benefit sales. It behooves the growth hacker to stay as granular as possible with sales processes (to identify opportunities). The growth challenges we faced were related to the consumer's trust. Previous regimes at the company tried and failed at paid search, paid social, and old-fashioned PR (smiling and dialing).

This project was one of the fastest increases in growth for both program development and revenue that I've ever seen. We quadrupled the company's sales in less than two months by leveraging organic, social, and paid traffic channels. We were promoting a business-to-consumer widget that was a cool modern twist on an old established household product. They'd raised a plethora of money from a crowdfunding site. A slew of high-priced consultants and CMOs had been in and out of the organization, which was apparent by their use of four distinct analytics suites of tools. To reach for the stars is a noble goal, but to build momentum teams have to be unified.

At first the product was hard for people understand. After a few months of concerted effort between agency and client, the consumers couldn't get enough of the product. The spike in sales rapidly led to a backordered situation, which was both a blessing and a curse. We were told that the investors were not going to extend any lines of credit, so once cash was out, it was out. The stakes grew increasingly steep for this client and fortunately we came through for them with mostly organic traffic when marketing budgets got cut. We worked social media super hard seven days a week and pumped out at least two decent blog posts. The blogs were listicles and we spent the time to have really good-looking pictures. We were liberal at times with the gifs and the internet loved it.

Like many companies, they experienced some delays in manufacturing. A natural disaster caused a major part of the delay, so the response by people on social was kind (at first). Promises were made by the CEO and they felt sincere, because I believe they were. The company still needed to generate income while the delays were happening. Only one person worked in marketing for a very long time and more recently a social media manager had been brought in to alleviate the pressure.

We immediately shut down the spending on unused tools, ineffective ads, and vanity paid-search spending. There were glossy ads with no real call to action or offer tied to them. There were even ads for just the CEO that basically only seemed to indicate how great he was as a leader. Needless to say, the ads did not perform well and therefore failed to bring in revenue. Company data was also being shared quite frivolously; nobody in the marketing department even knew who owned the access to most tools. Eventually we found out that several previous consultants actually owned the logins. We also had to calm down an overzealous social media manager who was deleting Facebook comments and responding directly to trolls on Twitter (using the company handle).

Sometimes when social managers read comments about the company they're defending long enough, they start to take the attacks personally. In this case, the social media manager felt any negative comments on social meant a risk to his job. It was clear that he was simply spooked by a few of the comments and felt backed into a corner for some reason. We recommended someone more experienced (with the product) from customer support take over social comment monitoring and response. Things went more smoothly from that point on.

The organic program was nonexistent; it was hard to figure out who the company was and who it was about. There was zero information on the founder or the CEO of the company, and not even one picture of the office could be found on the public website. We had to email and ask for the address of the kick-off meeting because it was impossible to find, along with a phone number. I can only imagine how someone would feel if they'd bought a product from this company and had any kind of issue. The company was hiding from the very people it had taken funds from.

We came up with three distinct campaigns that we executed and then measured carefully. The first campaign was to showcase the modern design feats of the product and how it was outperforming its predecessor, the second was a loyalty discount for a new product, and the third was a contest to do silly things and then win free stuff. People love free stuff! The contest campaign outperformed the others 4 to 1 in terms of interest.

Lastly we started a very successful affiliate program that included key social and industry influencers. We were lucky to snare a few big industry names, which tipped the scales in terms of brand power. All endorsements used the #sponsored tag so that it was 100% transparent that both affiliate influencers and customer influencers were paid for the endorsements. We gave them custom tracking URLs so we could measure by campaign what was working and what was not. By associating this product with powerful and influential people, we were able to grow the company's social followings so quickly that all ads became unnecessary.

**Lesson Learned:** Help wherever it's needed, even if it starts with providing the path to cutting unnecessary expenses (if a company doesn't have the confidence to do that on its own). A slow and steady hand sends the tweets. When leveraging influencers, don't parade them about; treat them like a partner, which means hearing what they suggest. If they're being paid for their endorsement, make that clear.

# B2B Social Spice

This client had a business-to-business tool that helped manage web services. Sometimes individual consultants would purchase the tool, but very rarely. The previous regime had made a total mess of this client's marketing program. Creatives were painfully bad stock photos that appealed to nobody and hence were performing poorly. The first step was to clean things up and then we got to take a step out with our new site.

The last person in charge of PPC moved over to HTTPS, rightly so, but did not actually change the URLs in the ads console. Every landing page was served up, kinda, but with a broken stylesheet. The conversion rates were the worst we'd seen.

Catching that mistake quickly quite literally saved the organization quickly. They were just in the middle of closing a funding round and sales mysteriously started to tank. Questions were being asked and they needed to be answered quickly. The ousted CMO left a trail of digital dust in her wake.

I always take the time to check the physical URLs a company is putting out there, not what they send me. I click on the URLs in any and all social listings, consoles, website footers, etc. You'd be surprised how often things are broken or simply do not match up. It always pays to review what's physically being put out there on the web and also within any of the promotional tools used against what is believed to be out there.

When clients are not making money because of someone's malfeasance, it's typical to demand a quick result from the next regime walking in the door. For us, the quick win was spotting the bad landing page URLs because fixing that immediately improved conversions. The previous consultant also forgot to separate branded from nonbranded search within the Google paid search groups. It's lesson number one in paid campaigns to start big and then whittle things down. Always separate ad groups intelligently so that you're able to drive the spend down for the group. Once paid was conquered, we started reviewing the organic side of the house, which had issues too. Every meta description was the same; artwork was generic and tired. It seemed as though every picture was from a classic hackneyed B2B stock art site: handshakes, the "we are all enjoying ourselves sitting and bantering" shot, or a grid with a finger pointing to it (Figure 9-1). Companies often use this type of corporate stock art to convey a sense of professionalism or appear larger than they are. Quite often these types of stock corporate photos come with templates for WordPress website themes.

*Figure 9-1. An example of the classic finger or hands on a grid stock art shots. Credit: Shutterstock (http://shutr.bz/2mxUBDQ).*

We needed to change most of the visuals quickly while getting the site in compliance with modern web standards. An old Joomla installation made site updates difficult, so migration to a more modern tool had to happen. Once the artwork was updated to interesting images that were originally designed by a designer, the conversions improved exponentially in the first few days.

The ecommerce plugin solution they were using was wiping lead source data out entirely. All traffic showed up as "direct" and not available for 80% of sales. Both the cart solutions analytics and the website's analytics showed the same thing; our traffic was sourced as "unavailable/direct." This was a big problem! We escalated to the third party what was happening and it took several weeks to work things out. The issue was with the third-party shopping cart's site, but we were responsible for fixing it. Ultimately we had to use Google Analytics' tag manager to pass on the cookie data in the transfer between cart and site.

While this case has the earmarks of your classic case of SEO—clean it up and watch it grow marketing—that is not where we saw our best sales success.

The majority of the clientele for this client were developers in Silicon Valley. They needed to get inside the hearts and minds of the web development crowd, the people whose lives were less pleasant without this particular tool. It's very hard to share a developer with a B2B marketing website with traditional trappings like white paper downloads, ask an engineer, or a free webinar.

Because of our own proximity to this market, we knew that conferences for marketing people were taking the side stage to conferences targeting developers. Giant symposiums were forming around getting in front of the developer, face to face. Many more modern developer or maker conferences have areas for origami, crafting, or working with 3D printers (*http://bit.ly/2mXWadH*). Developers are given a community to call home and camaraderie at these events, so to interject into them takes finesse. Our approach was geek humor and general supportiveness. If someone complained to the conference about allergies, we would offer them a tissue. On social, we were like a cool buddy from high school that's always there for you, not a company trying to sell itself.

We began to attend more and more developer-focused conferences. The client trusted us after dramatically turning around sales, so we got to tweet for the client account. As a former web developer, there was a certain amount of kidding around I felt comfortable knowing I could do. We'd built up that trust, which is a beautiful thing. I knew my three-letter acronym (TLA) game was tight, so onward I tweeted. We discovered very, very early in analytics that on the days when we attended conferences the client's site received more leads. Developer leads! We were copied on all leads coming into the site with coded email addresses for filtering. By having insights into the lead flow, we could tell what was working and annotate quickly.

Our assets went from webinars to pushing more and more conferences in real life (IRL). Sometimes intricate tools are best sold to their niches with a human face and interaction or a little personality on Twitter. By being a good guest at the conference, we often received dozens of retweets and favorites. Ahead of the conference, we'd write a highlights piece with background information for particular panels that were targeted to us. One year at the popular event conference, hackathon, and startup competition TechCrunch Disrupt, we had our most significant traffic spike with thousands of views in just an hour. On the other side, we'd get a recap of the conference panel with embedded Tweets and get that going for the next day. Timeliness of content when tied to social and real-life events was our rocket ship ride to developer snaring.

LinkedIn was our secondary community for lead generation, which surprised us. Our experiences on LinkedIn were somewhat negative on the paid side after the company went public. LinkedIn's InMails had a painfully low click-through rate. We were told our results were poor because we had the wrong audience or we weren't paying enough. It doesn't inspire confidence to know that if you haven't gotten us money in the past that more money will lead to different results. In this case, organic optimizations, highly specialized content, and social promotion benefited the client far more than paid.

**Lesson Learned:** Know your audience. If at first you don't succeed, test and test again. Online success can almost always be boosted by coordinated offline activity. Don't follow convention; follow instincts.

# Dysfunction Junction

Sometimes the institutional goals are just a thin political charade. People often bring trouble from their personal lives into work; in this case, it ran rampant. This organization had a lot of things going for it internally, a decent product offering in a space that was exploding. This company was a B2B services industry platform that combined their software with consulting services. The end result for this company's customers was dramatic savings and increased sales efficiency. To onboard this company for a large enterprise was a no-brainer; they integrated with a good amount of services that were already out there.

We began this project with the excitement all new projects deserve. After studying everything, we had some very practical priority suggestions to get the ball rolling, like fixing broken links and improving the analytics instrumentation. All title attributes were the same for every single page of the website. They were passing traffic back and forth to subdomains for no real reason. It was a bit of a nest. But once we ran out of the recommendation zone, the trouble started.

There was no system for approval. Every tiny thing required ten conversations, all of which led back up to the top. Quickly it became clear that we had a bridge-and-troll situation. The VP was the only one who could approve any website change as low level as correcting broken link repair. There were multiple senior marketing managers who reported to the VP, yet none of them could approve anything with finality, not even a blog post. We made updates that we subsequently saw overwritten by the client on multiple occasions.

We provided endless useful suggestions and tried to mediate what were becoming difficult conversations. When consulting on an SEO project, it's a 100% great idea for both sides to make sure there's zero mystery where the time is going. People shouldn't have to pay for mystery. Sometimes organizations get super busy for a spell. When we eventually got a thumbs-up to proceed on the project's tasks, we took extra care to make sure it was all documented. There was no way we had their full attention. The VP of marketing was anxious to see results while simultaneously being unwilling to let us do what needed to be done.

We were putting ideas out there to fix problems that we found, like providing conversion-increasing design comps. Our layouts highlighted their product more succinctly. We created stronger calls to action. What we actually managed to get implemented on the homepage showed almost instant organic benefits. We spelled out our strategy, but it wasn't being heard. The person who brought us in was powerless and eventually every conversation devolved into, "OK, I will talk to _____." We were dancing around an elaborate system of senseless roadblocks. This was an increasingly untenable situation unlike any I've ever encountered in my career.

The content, design updates, analytics, and layout changes we made to the site started to help increase the organic traffic. Then the PR consultant secured a hit in a major news outlet. We did a small social campaign at the same time, which was unrelated. Unfortunately, the PR consultant forgot to ask for links back to the company so none of the press hits contained links to the homepage. We identified that the traffic burst in analytics was from our campaign, not the press.

Because of the press hit, the client refused to believe that the traffic was from us, despite having the analytics in front of them displaying where the traffic came from. We were not hired for PR but seemed to be involved with it, because our influencer contacts ran deeper than the other resources engaged. The constant content and PR discussion led us away from SEO as a primary task. Scope creep is a tangible issue to watch out for in any consulting project and it always takes the search program off track. The general drama running rampant in this organization accounted for much of the business not getting handled, so eventually it became time to move on.

When people coming together on a project are not operating with common goals (in good faith), it's not worth the risk to continue. It came out a few years later that there was some corruption within the company that led to quite a bit of investigation by press.

**Lesson Learned:** When there is no remaining move to be made, the search battle is over. The goals have to line up across all relevant parties when you're building out a search program. It's normal to have a tiny bit of resistance when you are trying to physically change the innards of a marketing department, but too much resistance is a red flag. The marketing department's head did not allow so much as a blog post to go live without approval, and we were never going to win.

# Social Success!

This was the case of a popular online content site, respected amongst the community of tech and on par with major leading business publications. We helped them to find revenue online in a time when online content publishers were struggling to monetize social. Their industry awards drove a lot of revenue for the company as did their live conferences and local events. This project was ultimately a success because social media drove event registrations and award submissions.

This project started when their existing digital agency took down the Facebook page for violating terms of service by using some automated tool. The tool was supposed to enhance reporting and publishing, but it was also untested. While tools are tremendously important to an SEO's success, they can also lead to his or her downfall. They were fired for this very public and costly error. A significant amount of the magazine's traffic came from Facebook. In times of adversity, people often revert back to what they know. They understandably felt like letting anyone else handling social was a bad idea. After this experience, there was very little trust for vendors and that was the first mountain we had to climb. We summited and were the ones who got the page back up.

We didn't do anything fancy to get the site restored; we simply followed the process for dispute. It took three full days, but we got it up permanently. It's very tempting when you're faced with a difficult failure to want to call someone and force a solution. With the larger tools, it's always more reliable to follow the process they outline, and only escalate if that doesn't work.

To gain trust, we did the work and earned it. We scoured the web for future reputation issues or failures for performance. We studied their data to identify which marketing activities were working and which were not. While the publication was financially successful, they had extensive brand-leaking all over the web. Nobody was monitoring the name.

A dozen or so groups on LinkedIn had the magazine's name with different versions of the logo. The landing pages they were using for events did not even have the company site in the logo. All assets built for them by the previous agency were done on the previous agency's properties, not theirs. They were charging the client an astronomical rate to house this content (bitter divorce).

We stopped the bleeding and migrated all relevant content and registration to the page with a better CMS hitched up. Previously they were using a popular open source CMS system that had few associated fees until you took into account the human cost to maintain it. We switched them to a more robust system that required less management, so staff was freed up to build rather than maintain the site.

Fixing the LinkedIn groups took a little more time. We started by picking the largest group that anyone within the organization still had access to. We reported the groups that were rogue or untended to. They also had a record amount of Google+ pages. It took some time to track down ownership and close them out. The only way to get prominence for the LinkedIn group was to turn on the spigot. We posted every single article that came out on the group and used the extensive email list to invite the selected people to the group. Over the course of a few months, we had over 50,000 followers in the group and it was very clear to anyone searching for them that this was the correct group. They also had a LinkedIn company page, which we updated to have a more official presence.

We waited for their annual announcement of the top rankings for the companies they were researching that year to test out our theory about how to get into the LI headlines. I'd researched and tested with some other posts for another client and happened to figure out the formula. We repeated this for the client. Prior to the creation of LinkedIn Pulse, it was a great feat for publishers to get their links in the LI news headlines. We experimented and figured out the right combination of sharing content from individuals, groups, and private messages. Within the company, we coordinated the sharing of the awards both publicly and privately. The results were that they got featured in the LinkedIn news carousel for an entire day. It's unfortunate that the news carousel no longer exists; LinkedIn Pulse took over. Big sites always want to host content, not refer it out.

All emails were sent with the social badges, landing pages, and registration pages, too. We tweeted for them at live events and coached staff on how to do this. Eventually social media became a key component of their event strategy and was equal to other forms of traffic on the website. When it was award season again, we drove application signups by utilizing social media ads. With email addresses and retargeting options available for the ads, it was the best value. We also tweeted at individual companies with significant social reach to congratulate them.

**Lesson Learned:** Never give away your content without benefit. Experimentation leads to new knowledge, which can then be used for traffic gain. Diversified strategies are generally the best; just because something is working now doesn't mean it will forever. The strongest long-term strategy is to never form a dependency on one lead source. Yes, you can milk it as long as it lasts—but wells tend to run dry. Keep challenging yourself to find new strategies. Always maintain autonomy.

# CHAPTER 10

# Uncharted Search Frontiers

As our connectivity and technology increases, so will the importance of how we present ourselves digitally. We have to think beyond platforms and traditional search engines and begin moving towards infinite exchanges between experiences. *Omni-channel* is the new expected level for marketing programs. Nearly everything in our lives in and outside the home takes place on screens now, whether it's catching the bus, checking the weather, or finding your eye doctor's office.

Futurists envision a world where digital technology streams all around, shaping our nonvirtual existence for the better. People will always need help to find what they want, in search engines, apps, social networks, or possibly their own glasses. Search will most definitely extend beyond the devices we're carrying and using today. Cars have WiFi; soon they will contain Bluetooth everything *and* drive themselves.

## Embracing Expansive Realities

Gadgets and platforms like virtual reality (VR) will create unique challenges for the SEO professional. SEO will migrate beyond the concept of a screen or search engine and become part of life. Search has already become ingrained in our daily lives in a way that could mean the difference between life and death. Devices are connected to each other and where there's connection and WiFi plus processors in action, there's *search*. Mobile phones offer location-based experiences that are increasingly different than the norm, some of which can augment reality. It is left up to the cutting-edge SEO to cultivate new strategies to capture the expanded internet realities.

It's imperative for us to know how to find new information as members of society, or we inevitably risk getting left behind. For a small business, lack of access to inform or change what appears in search could create major problems at any time. Search pros will get left behind if they do not anticipate what's next; change is the most built-in part of the job. If you fear or dislike change, SEO may not be the field for you, at least not long term.

We will continue to consume more and more information with some type of virtual or augmented reality enhancement. Adobe (*https://adobe.ly/2lPDjgL*) states that the number of consumers in America that allow apps to access their phone's GPS to personalize their experience increased from 49% in 2013 to 58% in 2014. I would expect that to continue (*http://bit.ly/2mxXxjF*). More and more users are showing that they want to engage in location-specific experiences.

Emerging search devices that have been launched at the popular CES conference (*http://www.ces.tech*) range from the smart TV and smart watches to smart shoes and underpants. What *smart* means doesn't really always makes sense, but it almost always seems to include some type of connectivity between devices. By 2018, smart watches alone will move 100 million units or more. By 2018, over 250 million (*http://bit.ly/2mORBDj*) smart wearables will be in use, 14 times more than in 2013. Beacons are delivering real-time product and service messaging through Apple's iBeacon, Google Eddystone, and Facebook Beacons. Users will expect more contextual content such as discounts and coupons at live concerts or events. Couponing and incentives will become part of the event experience

---

### Pokémon Go

In the summer of 2016, a viral phenomenon known as Pokémon Go captured the imagination of the United States. Waves of people downloaded the app and ran around random places willy-nilly. The users went to parks, cemeteries, and all sorts of places in droves, feverishly (*http://bit.ly/2lxjsI1*).

As content creators, there were hundreds of Pokémon-themed blog posts and juicy blogs put out. Empires formed almost overnight. The Pokémon Go craze was linked to such unbelievable things like bolstering the Canadian government worker's pension fund (*http://bit.ly/2mOTEaw*) or murder (wrong place, wrong time). These wide-ranging events resulting from one game seem improbable.

The game became the largest augmented reality app of all time (that summer) and almost surpassed Twitter's user base in just a few weeks. Then it tanked just as quickly. But during that short time, augmented reality helped build a fast empire in that it generated massive paid revenue for multiple companies in terms of search opportunity.

---

*Augmented reality* (AR) is technology that enhances the user's perception of reality through computer-generated sensory input in a real-world environment. AR has been creeping into many areas of our lives, from the lines superimposed on the screen when watching a football game to the heads-up displays that can now be found in motorcycle helmets and new cars. Augmented reality crept into social with Snapchat, but maybe maps were a form of AR as well.

Marketing exists anywhere there is a screen. For those who are willing to take notice, AR offers exciting new possibilities when it comes to search. It could look something like this: a person searching for a doctor through their wearable device does a Google search and gets a hit from someone that left an AR marker with a review and star rating of a medical practice earlier in the week.

The whole notion of a cardboard virtual-reality headset seemed far-fetched not that long ago. Now all you need to experience VR is a mobile phone, an app, and a compatible cardboard viewer (literally a piece of cardboard). When I first tried out a cardboard virtual reality headset, it was so weird—yet it worked. The cardboard viewers are available for less than $20, making VR and AR-accessible worlds within reach for the masses. The smartphone has been toggled into many different types of wearable computing products that include virtual reality and augmented alike.

Traditional advertisements can no longer offer the same impact as VR ads will. Immersion gives consumers a more meaningful experience. VR monetization revenues are expected to reach $5 billion dollars by 2019, conservatively. Economically speaking, VR could also *create* billions in spending over the next ten years. As an industry, VR stands to benefit those working in marketing at any level.

Hearing aids and noise-cancelling wireless headphones are starting to evolve and now have tiny supercomputers in them. The top manufacturers claim you can tune in to your music, but also have normal conversations during concerts or tune out the noise around you. Soon we will also be able to receive all types of notifications (email, text, alarms, etc.) through voice (and privately too if you're using earbuds). Even though it's not a screen, one can imagine the marketing opportunities that lie therein.

Companies across the globe are running virtual simulations as a part of employee training. In fact, some schools are already planning lessons in VR (Figure 10-1). There are schoolchildren now taking virtual field trips. When consumers look to headsets for entertainment, experiences, and information, companies will need to be there.

VR has historically been associated with gaming, but there have been dramatic advancements into other industries. While the opportunity for the gaming ecosystem is unlimited, practical applications have also flourished. Time Magazine (*http://ti.me/ 2lV42JS*) said VR is the technology that is going to change the world. The numbers are astonishing: the industry is projected to hit $6 billion by 2018. The SEO industry, much like the medical field, will be invariably improved through the use of VR technology. One example of industry expansion is Embodied Labs' (*http://huff.to/ 2mYKdSO*) VR program "We are Alfred," which provides medical students with the opportunity to feel what it is like to be elderly. Another example is Solis (*http://www.solisvr.com*), the portable VR solution for medical eldercare.

*Figure 10-1. VR workshop. Credit: UploadVR. (http://www.uploadvr.com)*

Expanded virtual realities create an opportunity for shoppers to look at actual products, and virtually feel them in their hands prior to purchasing. I've actually test-driven a car, hunted for dinosaurs, and ridden a roller coaster using VR. We expect the VR industry to explode, which will translate to greater profits for SEO professionals that recognize the technology for the power it provides and affords their clients.

The challenge is greater than ever before to be an SEO, but so are the rewards. Input methods for search were *always* more than text, but now we're dealing with different planes of existence and media. It is vital for search professionals to take a step back and reassess everything. It's hard to fully understand how the methodologies change in terms of SEO, but they change because the inputs do. AR markers are largely based on images so we must think about how to optimize them in descriptions, attributes within tags, etc. Also, with AR, location will be of the utmost importance. We've seen the differences in local mobile versus nonlocal desktop search results; the differences will only continue to increase.

Augmented reality has the potential to influence almost every aspect of our lives as our existences become omni-screen.

# Interfaces Galore!

We are kids in an unfolding candy store. Changes in our input methods for search have created an interesting twist when it comes to reviews of products or services provided by a business. No longer would a one-star review be accompanied by a short statement on why the person was dissatisfied. An entire video or image can be included with some sites. There are hotel review sites like TripAdvisor that allow users (hotel guests) to post what the property *actually* looks like. Online relevance coupled with the social sharing of life's experiences have meant a field day for marketers. This is just the beginning.

We're not in text-land anymore, Dorothy. Many top SEOs are creating not just focused text but also images, gifs, video, and even meme content to be distributed across a litany of sites.

Think about how you can take those new ideas and market them to the masses on *all the screens where eyeballs roam*. Think of search problems multidimensionally, beyond the current limitations of what is available. As is so common in the search game, additional inputs and types of data add a new layer of challenges but also opportunities. VR and AR together create new chances to link to relevant content or to deep link from mobile apps. As the new ecosystem develops, the opportunities will be endless. Similarly, for businesses that do not jump on board, it becomes harder to successfully compete. This means it's not good enough to be just found anymore—we have to be fun, too. Usability is a serious function of search domination and ecommerce. *Gamification* became a way of life for mobile marketing; things have to just need to work the way we want.

> Design is not just what it looks like and feels like. Design is how it works.
>
> —Steve Jobs (*http://nyti.ms/2lPGGUZ*), Visionary and CEO of Apple Computer, Inc.

Our mobile lives are 100% lived on the grid; the inner workings of our present is recorded and our future will be predicted. As marketers, we don't yet fully understand all that we can do with the data that mobile phones collect. There are tools that push us to deeper understanding of mobile usability, but they are in their infancy. It's OK. AI can improve our lives and it will also improve certain processes if we create them with those goals. I see AI as an opportunity to help us see things we cannot but also to process large pieces of information simultaneously and effortlessly in order to make predictions. There are always those who fight for technology and those who will fight against new ideas in general.

There are both utopian and dystopian AI narratives, according to Professor Shannon Vallor (*http://www.shannonvallor.net*). She suggests that to assuage AI fears, we should avoid the "walks like a duck" fallacy in which we start to view the technology as *some form of humanity* because it walks, talks, and moves like us. Professor Vallor also has wisely surmised that wisdom leads to intelligence, which leads to knowledge. Just like with coding, we can *separate the concerns* into the following categories when it comes to understanding AI:

- Imagination
- Experiments

There's no doubt that we will see changes in search based on artificial intelligence beliefs. It's staggering. Modern SEO has yet to skim the surface of what predictive algorithms will do to search. Products will be layered upon products wherever the user's eyeballs go, and products *will* evolve. Where there could be other applications for AI is where it gets really interesting: we'll see changes in determining real-life threats like cyber crime and the hacking of our personal data—and even our governments. Technological agents of the robot variety will be able to find unpredicted patterns with increasing complexity and sweep for emerging threats sometimes known as black swans or bad actors.

---

## Random Interfaces: From Smart Watches to Beacons

You're probably asking yourself, how does a smart watch relate to SEO? Search is possible on each device that contains a microprocessor and connects to the internet. The *Pebble* is essentially a little computer that connects to the internet via your phone's bluetooth. The Pebble has an open API.

Programmers can search for and develop apps on the Pebble platform. This relationship creates a bridge every marketer can cross because it's another channel of communication to reach people. Right now it's mostly apps, but soon it could be voice command and gestures as well.

We know that SEO will continue to evolve through different devices and platforms. I believe that search will become largely powered by voice through search assistants and mobile phones. The inputs and outputs are changing for search; the data layers are being mapped but cannot yet be understood or correlated.

---

If VR expands as rapidly as expected, it will mean a major shift in how companies communicate and market themselves. Today, the push is to optimize for mobile and apps. We must think of tomorrow. Slow adoption means missed opportunities in a market that is rising at a meteoric rate.

There was a time when no business would have been caught dead without a yellow pages ad. Today it would be nearly unheard of for a business to not have a mobile website appear for smartphones and tablets. In five years, it may be similarly rare for there to be a business without VR content for shoppers.

# Machine Learning

The future of search means learning to stop worrying and love the machine. Machine learning (ML) is not new as a field. It was first proposed by Arthur Samuel in 1959 (*http://www.geeksforgeeks.org/machine-learning-introduction*) as "the ability to learn without being explicitly programmed." ML is where machines can predict various events using data models. Data models learn from, well, *data*. Data is being produced from all sides by the petabyte. Machine learning is more of a statistics-based approach to AI versus a symbolic computation, which a lot of people are accustomed to. You might be able to tell an ML practitioner from their strange lingo, such as terms like "SoftMax," "skip-gram," "bag of words," and "one-hot vector."

Thanks to moves ahead in ML and AI, the capabilities of Siri, Alexa, and Cortana are more mature than earlier iterations. The digital assistive technologies are able to interpret and respond to much longer, multipart, and specific queries. Multipart queries are something voice assistants were unable to do just 12 months ago.

*Deep learning* is a mix between a buzzword and a concept. The *learning* part is straight out of AI research, and refers to neural nets. *Neural nets* are data structures that loosely mimic physical neurons in order to simulate brain-like functioning. Recent computing advances such as cheaper graphic processing units (GPUs) have enabled ever-larger neural nets, stacked in layers, and even layers of layers. That's where the *deep* comes from. Of course, since the field has been around for a long time, the inside joke is that deep learning is really deep marketing.

We dream of machines coming to their own conclusions, yet we fear it all at the same time. The funny thing is that ML is not new, nor is it truly automated. Humans still need to engage heavily in training ML projects (for now). Self-directed algorithms are a booming field of research, but humans still have to set the parameters.

In search marketing, we're constantly looking at how people try to find things they need. Search algorithms have always been and always will be at the core of AI research. The saying "The medium is the message" was one (partial) example of people going "Oh yeah! The power lies in *controlling* the information!"

> You will never reach your destination if you stop and throw stones at every dog that barks.
>
> —Winston S. Churchill

In George Orwell's *1984*, history was constantly rewritten so that the victors would always find the "right" information in a search. Studying your potential *searchee* means following more than keywords; it's looking at different places and formats. Recent research data indicates that voice search (*http://bit.ly/2lVhdul*) and longer, question-style queries are dramatically on the rise.

When it comes to thinking about what's on the rise, we have to think about how much money corporations are willing to spend in order to be there. The big players don't like leaving their money to chance. Google has deals in place with Facebook and Twitter amongst countless others. There's always going to be a part of the game that is paid. The growth-hacking go-getter type of SEO practitioner must always lust a little for paid. Time spent on site has typically been longer for organic traffic because the trust is there. People greet ads with more skepticism.

Now it's not so clear to people what's real and what's not. Random real-life incidents between strangers have occurred all around the world because of what's been put out on social.

---

## Spotting Fake News

We've all fell for a headline that turns out to not be true—celebrities pronounced dead, pure political propaganda, or maybe that new vitamin that causes you to *immediately* lose that unwanted belly fat. This fake content trend is poison to brains and our ability to understand what's happening in the world. Years ago, we laughed at the made-up news and *rightly* called sources like the Weekly World News (*http://usat.ly/2my5XYb*) "tabloids."

Because of our peers and various algorithms in the background quietly deciding our preferences, we have come to assume a certain level of couth. Unfortunately the web will always stay uncouth, so we must find a workaround: ourselves. By trusting our instincts and developing mechanisms to report fraud (aside from Snopes (*http://www.snopes.com*)) we can move towards a more truth-filled world.

To spot fake news, consider the following factors:

1. Examine the physical URL. Is it actually CNN.com or a weird version of that? Check the spelling and domain extension carefully (e.g., CNNN.com or CNN.us).
2. Is the headline decidedly sensational?
3. Was the news written on a site that lacks the whiff of editorial oversight? Do you see any evidence of research or supporting links?
4. Consider the source and its validity (i.e., did you read it on The Onion (*http://www.theonion.com*)?).
5. Are you seeing this news as a result of clicking on an ad or via a social network? Then be twice as scrutinizing.
6. Did you click on it under a news article with the headline "from the web" (Figure 10-2)?

---

From the Web                                    Sponsored Links by Taboola

**The Gmail Trick that Google**      **Now You Can Track Your Car**    **Not dead yet: Seven brands**
**Doesn't Want You to Know**          **Using Your Smartphone**         **hanging on by a thread**
Boomerang for Gmail                   Trackr Bravo                      Campaign US

*Figure 10-2. Taboola, Outbrain, and other services offer native ads that are commonly used on news sites.*

A query that combines multiple disparate sources into one combined search result is known as a *federated search*. This can sometimes also be called a *distributed database* (*http://bit.ly/2nNOV5x*) search or a *universal search*. In the future, all searches will be federated searches. Let's analyze why this is. First of all, consider that all networks have some *theoretical value*. How much that value is depends on a slew of factors. A major component in this valuation is the connectedness of the network, as in how well it meshes with itself and other (useful) networks. Secondly, smaller niche domain databases will become increasingly more connected. Think about how tightly integrated search engines are to airlines through sites like Travelocity, Kayak, and the like. Also consider that all of your contacts are a small network, as is all that data you're generating via your present and future IoT devices. Just for kicks, you can then add in your fitness information, your diet information, and the list goes on and on. There is only so much data to be gleaned from public websites, but more knowledge can be gained from rolling in the other networks to get more *context* about the world at large.

Networks come together to form a giant mathematical graph, and algorithms exists to allow computer scientists and analysts to attack it with Graph Theory. Special graph databases store these special interconnected structures. Previous generations of hardware couldn't handle the volume! One was incubated at Facebook, yet another at Google. These graphs can have as many as billions of nodes and can be queried in real time. They can also help visualize the structures in the data, and provide the large amounts of data needed for a large machine-learning pipeline. They can also store a large amount of unstructured data quickly, which is also useful for data collection. DBpedia is a one such publicly available data set, obtained from mining Wikipedia (and other sources). More on this later.

Social network graphs tend to be part of things known as *Small World networks*. This refers to the fact that most social networks tend to be tightly clustered self-selected groups that probably don't break down into traditional advertising areas for targeting.

Data visualization tools can also help highlight structures in the data. Being able to coalesce these connected groups out of the raw data is a valuable marketing skill to expand your reach. What if you could pick up emotional biases on data? That's actually how sentiment analysis works and it will become an important tool for real-time trend analysis. Eventually, this will become sentiment predictors although they probably won't get much better than humans, since trend prediction is similar to weather forecasting. We're really only in the nascent phases of sentiment analysis. Dissecting one simple sentence requires advanced logic mapping (Figure 10-3). Most analysis is based on things like Twitter feeds, but later we can expect more advanced sites like news and content sites. Sentiment has only begun to skew search results.

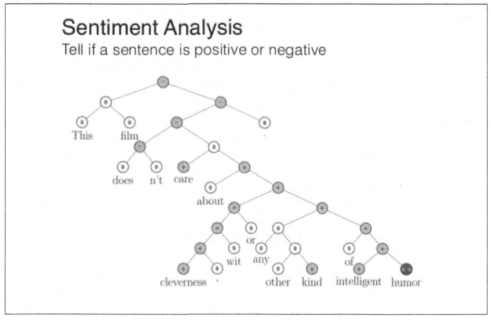

*Figure 10-3. An example sentence diagram. Credit: Hacking Human Language (http://bit.ly/2nhVlNu) (PyData London, slide 16).*

How do these programs actually learn? They're trained. Tools are becoming easier to use so that soon anyone will be able to slap together a pedantic "AI solution." Even in unsupervised learning, you have some kind of goals. The hardest part of machine learning is supervising your algorithms: aiming for convergence, not divergence. Also, we must ensure we're not converging on the *wrong* solution, which can be harder to tell. It's almost as though if you don't keep an eye your machines, they will spend half the day smoking in the bathroom instead of doing any actual work.

Ensemble algorithms work to combine different types of more basic algorithms into bigger building blocks for higher accuracy. There are even subtypes with pithy names like *boosting* and *bagging*. This culminates on a large scale into things like contextual audience targeting (i.e., Google display network), in which you choose topics based on keywords, and it can decide from those keywords how to target ads based on contextual clues and cutting-edge linguistics algorithms.

Just as an example, let's talk about word vectors. The word2vec (*https://deeplearn ing4j.org/word2vec*) tool is a popular open source program based on a set of linguistic models. You can use it to process a corpus containing thousands (or millions) of natural language documents and it will try to learn the relationships among the words in the documents. It represents these as vectors, and can use vector math to do traditional SAT-like analogy problems. For instance, in one example the authors asked a word model, "As king is to man, what is to woman?" The answer was, of course, "Queen." It was such a successful concept that it has given rise to corollary concepts such as paragraph vectors to compare meanings of paragraphs, document vectors, and even *thought vectors*. The latter is a concept championed by Geoffrey Hinton (*http://bit.ly/2nvZcXN*), the prominent deep-learning researcher for both the University of Toronto and Google. Google is using vectors based on *natural language* to improve its search results.

## Ethical Data Science

What will we SEOs do in the future? We will all be aspiring data scientists or actual data scientists with statistical and database-modeling experience. What responsibilities will data scientists have in the future? Responsibility isn't only up to data scientists, but also anyone handling analytics for organizations. Controlling data for an organization often means you're controlling finances as well; this is a great responsibility.

There are often accidental biases in the data. In my favorite slightly apocryphal tale of ML lore, researchers were tasked with training a model to determine whether a picture was a dog or a wolf. They started with the test data, used proper techniques, prepared their model, then set it off to train. It's not unusual in research settings to train jobs for durations of many days or even weeks. As such, the researchers were glad to discover that their model seemed able to predict the difference with almost 100% accuracy. Their hopes were dashed when it was discovered that the machines had learned from the many pictures they had seen: wolves tended to have snowy backgrounds, whereas dogs did not. They had accidentally trained a machine to recognize a white background. While that may be a funny story, the implications of this are definitely serious (*http://for.tn/2mXWPvH*) and should not be taken lightly.

More evidence continues to accumulate that models are being deployed with weaknesses in areas such as discrimination in hiring practices, or even police work. Even if the individuals running the program aren't shady, the data might be. The program will mirror the likenesses of the implicit biases it receives. Another example could be a prediction model trying to anticipate which customers will buy a toy so that we can best market to them. This might result in marketing computers or other science toys to only boys. Not only would this be a tragedy for young women, but also a catastrophic market failure (missing 50% of your potential customers). Fortunately, you can combat bias by being aware of it and always knowing your model and data.

What is the opposite of *creep*? It's not *cool*, it's *empathy*. Some might even say it is empathy bordering on respect. Empathy and respect for what, you might ask. The answer is your users (not just clients), as well as the safety of your data and the individuals it belongs to. When it comes down to it, the data points are all people, just like yourself. Your data might not seem imperatively significant, but big data is made up of all kinds of "little data" that you might be very concerned to see out-and-about in the world. Data might include social security numbers, medical records, credit information, and purchase habits. Sometimes the information can be assembled and correlated to produce a much larger story. It might not even take an AI to reverse-engineer this information out. As such, always consider the privacy of your sources.

Not only is it rude to gossip, but it may potentially become illegal to let information escape in untold ways. Laws cover this differently in different geographical areas. Know your local regulations. Are you worried about adjusting the data to fit your own conclusions? Here's what to do:

1. Use proper sampling techniques.
2. In a machine learning model, split your test and data sets to make sure there aren't *any* unknown correlations.
3. Correlation does not imply causation.
4. Practice responsible reduction of dimensionality.

Don't just throw your hands up and say it's too complex. Map it out. A good data practitioner will always understand their own models.

### Random Future Thoughts

As a Futurist, certain trends seem inevitable to me. Here are a few random future thoughts of how we can expect search technology to shape our lives in the near term.

- Cars will have cognitive and search capabilities, spanning far beyond GPS.
- VR adoption will be massive, but it could take a while to get over creep factors.
- AI is always going to freak out certain people.
- Moore's Law will be further gamed.
- Machine learning will get less human-dependent, but never all the way.

# A Moonshot

SEO and growth hacking have converged, *if ever* they were that far apart. Data science looms in the background, coming closer. Despite a data modeling background, it's not *exactly* data science to perform SEO, but it's close. I've taken to calling myself a "growth scientist," because of the constant experimentation and general practice of scientific methods in the SEO field of business. The tactics have spread far and wide across a multitude of practice areas. Emerging platforms have created a climate where development is not always necessary. The great division in our search practice will continue to widen between the technical and nontechnical SEOs. It's the Wild, Wild West! This is an exciting time to fight for search dominance (or any web attention at all).

Social media is not a natural part of the SEO environment, but given that the user experience is changing, search engines have started to favor popular social media updates in the top sections of SERPs. Also, partnerships have been forged and money exchanged. SEOs must mind the relationships of the big search fish. Meanwhile, social media has heralded the introduction of *social commerce*, a spicy enterprise indeed! *Forbes'* Baldwin Cunningham (*http://bit.ly/2n7NhuX*) espouses the effect that social commerce has on marketing and sales and driving the two together. I have seen cases where social media has almost entirely eliminated the need for a standalone website. If this trend continues, it will begin changing the entire focus of an SEO strategy onto social media alone. He also points out that 59% of all online retail browsing is done on mobile, which is responsible for 15% of ecommerce sales. Such a low percentage of sales indicates that there is a significant amount of opportunity to drive sales, which is the *ultimate* purpose of a growth marketer.

Square (*https://squareup.com*) and other mobile payment services seek to change the mobile payment conversion numbers. Retailers only seek to win from more agile payment systems. Many small retailers can sell wherever they are. About a decade ago, pop-up (*http://bit.ly/2mRtAJ1*) stores became a popular thing. Now, mobile technology makes it even easier. Kiosks could make a cogent difference in local SEO.

Experiences will continue to be personalized and optimized. There will be a service for everything and everything in a service, because mobile allows for it. Sprig (*https://www.sprig.com*) brings healthy gourmet to your house on-demand as easily as pizza; Freshly (*https://www.freshly.com*) does fresh food delivery weekly. Rinse (*https://www.rinse.com*) (formerly Washio) picks up your dirty clothes and washes and mends them on-demand; Lugg (*https://lugg.com*) moves your stuff on-demand. R. Buckminster Fuller's dream of a shared space utopia has started to happen, quite literally. Airbnb (*https://www.airbnb.com*), Homeaway (*https://www.homeaway.com*), and other services are making unused space used. You can now optimize for search and conversions for guests of your own micro-hotel (guest room). Appearance in the search panopticon matters. Reviews are life or death now and a phonebook is a distant dream of the past.

The types of content we create as marketers should steer away from clickbait, and propaganda (i.e., the things that make the web industry weak). Promoting garbage helps nobody. What influences us negatively in our online experiences also leads us to *silo ourselves* online. When we narrow our focus of attention, we get weak informationally. I've said a myriad of times in this book to diversify. The problem with silos is that they will eventually become information-less tombs. Adam Scott, developer and educator for the Consumer Financial Protection Bureau (*http://www.consumerfi nance.gov*), discusses the concept of how technology can enable us but also simultaneously leave people behind.

Adam Scott's four ethical core principles (*http://oreil.ly/2mDPIpf*) are:

- Web applications should work for everyone.
- Web applications should work everywhere.
- Web applications should respect a user's privacy and security.
- Web developers should be considerate of their peers.

Huzzah! I love these concepts, which hold true for search efficacy. The future of our data integrity depends on the practice of responsible data management and analysis. Big networks that hold too much power have the ability to influence the world negatively. By remembering the concept of accessibility on every level of what we do, we can find a way towards common ground.

It's possible that one day pricing models for ads will adapt to what's happening in reality as a different means to determine renumeration for display ads. There could be multiple payouts spread across advertisers. The ad industry might just standardize like shipping containers did in the 1960s. How will it work when cars have search? Self-driving cars? Will fast-food places throw in a few pennies every time you let the car take you through the drive-through?

Our relationship is changing on every level, from data to platforms. The SEOs who do not abandon less linear ideals will perish.

> It's always time to question what has become standard and established.
>
> —David Bowie

SEO as a term feels like it may have come and gone; maybe growth hacking has too. Whatever we decide to call what we're doing, it's clear that search is not a fad: it is actually a science. Science! Search is more methodical today than ever and it has become deeper over the years. We're knee-deep in data, so as practitioners we get to question everything because we can measure it and prove the things we want to prove. Data scientist doesn't necessarily feel right as a title for what we do because they're expected to have a thorough background in statistics, not just data modeling alone. Marketing will only keep moving towards the technical so it's time we use a new term: growth science.

Scientists are merely humans who come from a variety of backgrounds to practice the scientific method out in the field. We should aspire to transcend into growth science. Wikipedia defines the scientific method (*http://bit.ly/2nic8QK*) as "a body of techniques for investigating phenomena, acquiring new knowledge (*http://bit.ly/2nNCWVp*), or correcting and integrating previous knowledge." SEO is a continuous go-round of investigation, experimentation, and information gathering. If we boil it all down, search is the evolving door to change. It's how we get there when we're lost.

In terms of SEO, ASO, and general search engine efficacy, the commonality is they seek to measure and/or create growth. This is the niche for those of us who are emerging as growth scientists. She (or he) strives above all to seek new methods, not magic, to bring new insights into the data. What does a growth scientist practice? It's *Scientific Search Optimization* (SSO), which has some defined parameters:

*Hypothesis*
Study data and form conclusions. Take guesses for what you think might be happening and posit a theory.

*Methodical*
The method to determine the results was determined beforehand, based on the hypothesis. For example: adding additional schema to the pictures on my homepage will draw more organic search traffic.

*Provable*
The results are validated, given the inputs.

*Reproducible*
If the test was re-run the conclusions would be the same.

Growth scientists should also embrace open standards. As data sets become larger and toolsets become more integrated, open standards and open source software are important to maintain transparency. Freedom for independent toolset integrations can help prevent vendor lock-in. This all suggests a future path for the discipline of SEO: it's SSO.

Just as with science in any other field of expertise, only public experiments contribute to a collective body of knowledge, and improvement to the growth discipline. To truly earn the title of growth scientists, we must also grow into a community of fellow practitioners who share our results, discuss our latest experiments, and peer review our results.

*Magic is not a method, hope is not a strategy.*

# Index

third-party content hosts, 110
thumbnails, 121
time-based offers, 107
TL;DR (too long, don't read), 102
tools
    all-in-ones
        Customer.io, 60
        Eloqua, 60
        Hubspot, 59
        Marketo, 59
        Pardot, 59
        selecting, 58, 109
    analytics
        A/B vs. multivariate tests, 53
        ClickTale, 58
        CrazyEGG, 57
        goals of tracking, 53
        Google Analytics, 54
        Hotjar, 58
        KISSmetrics , 57
        Mixpanel, 57
        New Relic, 57
        Optimizely, 56
        privacy concerns, 58
        selecting, 86
        situations analyzed, 54
    automation
        auto linking tools, 68
        Google Alerts, 68
        IFTTT, 68
        importance of scalability, 68
        SpyFu, 64
        Twitterfeed, 68
    content management systems
        benefits of, 69
        Drupal, 70
        Ghost, 69
        Joomla, 70
        Medium, 70
        Prismic, 69
        WordPress, 69
    vs. human ingenuity, 51, 71
    keyword research tools
        Google Keyword Planner, 64
        keyword goals, 63
        selecting, 75
        SEMrush, 64
        SpyFu, 64
        using, 80

providing feedback on, 52
research tools
    Scrapebox, 61
    selecting, 60
    Serpstat, 61
    website source data, 60
SEO diagnostic tools
    Chrome Developer tools, 62
    Majestic, 62
    proper application of, 62
    SEOptimer, 62
social tools
    Buffer, 65
    Cyfe, 67
    Famebit, 67
    Followerwonk, 67
    Hootsuite, 65
    login authentications, 66
    Pitchbox, 67
    Quintly, 67
    significance of social traffic, 65
    Simply Measured, 67
    Sprout Social, 66
    testing, 60, 123
tracking scripts, 118
traffic approximations, 48
trends, spotting, 25, 28-31
trust and transparency, building, 21, 74
Twig, 70
Twitch, 121
Twitterfeed, 68
typographical conventions, xiii

# U

unattributed data, 56
universal searches, 169
unstructured data, 139
untrusted data, 73
URL structure, 113, 118
usability, 112-115, 125, 132
user experience (UX), 112, 136
user interfaces (UI), 112
user-generated content (UGC), 27
Ustream, 121

# V

value, conveying, 107
Velvet Rope, 99
video handling, 120

Vimeo, 121
Vine, 121
virtual/augmented reality, 107, 162
voice commands, 130-132

# W

W3C, 35, 116
Watson, 127
wearable computing
    author's attempt at, ix
    spotting trends, 29-31
web forms, 19
Web standards, 35
website marketing
    author's discovery of, x
    competitive analysis of, 20
    page titles and descriptions, 110
    site architecture, 109, 118
    site canonicalization, 119
    site performance optimization, 114, 115, 118

site usability, 112-115
    viewing source data, 60, 85, 112
white hat SEO, 21
Whois, 21
widgets, 92
WordPress, 69, 71, 110, 122
Wordpress for AMP, 71
Wordtracker, 80
WP Engine, 110
WP Smush, 71

# Y

Yoast, 71
YouNow, 121
YouTube, 121

# Z

Zendesk, 110

## About the Author

**Anne Ahola Ward** is a Growth Scientist and the CEO of CircleClick Media, a leading digital agency and marketing lab in the Bay Area. As a Futurist through-and-through, Ward spent over 10 years mastering all things web development before transitioning into the nascent field of SEO. She quickly became an SEO trailblazer by applying her love of analytics to digital marketing. Anne was named as one of *Entrepreneur* magazine's 27 Top Masters of Marketing and PR that everyone can learn from. In 2015, Ward was invited to become an Influencer for the elite IBM Futurist program. She is a frequent conference speaker and has been recognized as a leading marketing expert by numerous publications. Her other interests include robotics and VR (Virtual Reality).

## Colophon

The animal on the cover of *The SEO Battlefield* is the steppe eagle (*Aquila nipalensis*), a bird of prey native to the vast steppes of eastern Europe and central Asia. During winter, steppe eagles migrate to Africa and southern Asia. They are mostly brown, with black tail feathers. Male steppe eagles can grow to 81 centimeters in length, while females are slightly larger.

The diet of steppe eagles consists mostly of carrion and small rodents, especially susliks, a type of ground squirrel also native to the Eurasian steppes. Because steppe eagles live in a flat grassland habitat, they build their nests on the ground. Unfortunately, this makes them vulnerable to habitat destruction. As more of the steppe has been converted to agricultural land, the population of the steppe eagle has declined, and they are now listed as endangered.

The steppe eagle is culturally significant to the people of central Asia. It appears on the flag of the modern nation of Kazakhstan and has been used in the symbols of Kazakh tribes for centuries. For the Kazakh people, the steppe eagle represents independence and freedom.

Many of the animals on O'Reilly covers are endangered; all of them are important to the world. To learn more about how you can help, go to *animals.oreilly.com*.

The cover image is from *Braukhaus Lexicon*. The cover fonts are URW Typewriter and Guardian Sans. The text font is Adobe Minion Pro; the heading font is Adobe Myriad Condensed; and the code font is Dalton Maag's Ubuntu Mono.